MW01614847

"I will never forget reading about this woman's experience. The author was able to put me in the room with her and the demon, and I could almost feel the terror and the fear in the woman's words as she questioned if this was how she would die. To say that I respect this individual for her courage and perseverance would be an understatement. She is a hero and her story is a testimony to gun safety and will educate many others as to maintaining a personal safety plan. If you have never held a gun, buy one and take a gun safety course. If you own a gun, follow the author's practice."

Lee A. Tindal, Summary Court Judge
South Carolina

"As a survivor of domestic abuse and subsequent PTSD, I can attest that the author's advice is well-founded and essential for living in a world that is increasingly uncertain and unsafe. Unfortunately, people – especially women - can no longer go about their lives with reasonable assurance that no one would want to do them harm. Today, education, vigilance, and preparedness are key to survival. I am grateful that the author had the courage to explore this woman's ordeal in order to write *Armed Survivor*, and I am very thankful the woman safely survived such a horrific experience."

Amy Lorenti, Graphic Designer
North Carolina

"This horrific account of one woman's experience is a page turner. The author takes a great effort to be exact in her research. The book was a severe warning to me and other women to be aware of your surroundings and to be prepared as possible for an assault. We have defensive driving courses; we need defensive tools and instincts to ward off a violent attack."

Charline Payne, Author and Poet
Georgia

"What a terrifying, horrific experience! The woman's bravery and mental control is to be commended. Her level-headedness is the key that allowed her to save her life. We are always told to remain calm in a life-threatening situation. That is almost impossible when the situation is as unpredictable and startling as the one described in this book. This woman has shown us that not allowing the perpetrator to feel the fear she was living, and to remain in control of her actions and responses, are necessary elements needed at all times when life-altering events occur. Fear is paralyzing! Had this woman responded in that manner and lost control she undoubtedly would not be here to give us an account of how she survived…we are grateful!"

Eleanor Taylor Adam, Consultant
Georgia

"Intense, unnerving, and thought-provoking! A must-read for every woman. The author covers important topics such as home defense and safety tips, gun ownership, all while telling a gripping story of survival. She is a hero."

Bettye Kelley, Business Owner
Georgia

"A young police officer who met the woman in the hospital after she survived her attack said to let him know when she wrote a book. He would share it with the women in his family. Here is a riveting read, not just for women, but for anyone who cares about U.S. immigration problems. This woman is still fighting back through an honest investigation into the circumstances that led an attacker to her door."

Tracy Kaminer, Educator
Virginia

"The author created a good flowing account of this woman's horrific ordeal while educating the reader on everything from gun control to the intricacies of the U.S. judicial systems. Readers will come to realize the psychotic thinking of a stalker and pure randomness in choosing the victim. I have been told many times that God only gives us what we can handle and I believe that this woman found that to be true. I sincerely hope that the author and this individual found this research into the many facets of the case cathartic."

Frances Hennelly, Writer
Georgia

"The author addresses a wide range of topics from women and guns, stalking, coping with Post Traumatic Stress Disorder, and home and self-defense suggestions. She then goes on to tackle bigger issues such as immigration and border control enforcement leading to a needed discussion on the Department of Homeland Security's role in detaining criminals. It's a timely read in this day and age of terrorism."

LePret Williams, Consultant
Alabama

"Survival is the name of the game. This story was riveting and should be read by men and women – a gift from the heart. The woman is a clever, brave, and an intuitive lady! I am lucky to know this courageous individual who I consider a warrior. The author of *Armed Survivor* addresses serious topics and raises important questions. I will be sure to recommend this read to my friends and family!"

Dr. Teresa Wilburn, Professor, Author,
Radio Talk Show Host, Counselor, Consultant
Georgia

The true story of how the Second Amendment
was all that stood between a woman and her attacker

ARMED
SURVIVOR

A stalker's
reign of terror finally
comes to an end.

CHRISTINE
GONZALES

Copyright

ARMED SURVIVOR
@ 2015 Published by author, Christine Gonzales, Ed.D.
South Carolina

ISBN-13:
978-0996251204 (College Path, LLC)
ISBN-10:
0996251200
ISBN eBook:
978-0-09962512-1-1

Cover and book design by KlearIdea.com

Copyright 2015 © College Path, LLC - All rights reserved. This book may not be duplicated in any way without the express written consent of the author. The information contained herein is for the personal use of the reader and may not be incorporated in any commercial programs or other books, databases, or any other kind of software without the permission of the publisher or author. Making copies of this book, or any portion of it, for any purpose other than your own, is a violation of the United States copyright laws.

To the Reader

You must ask the questions to find the answers. I wrote *ARMED SURVIVOR* to share the story of a very brave woman, offer tips for home/self-defense, note resources for victims of sexual assault, and address questions regarding immigration and homeland security.

The reader will follow a timeline of each character's life until the point where the two cross paths. The result of their interaction and the aftermath will make you think twice.

This story was inspired by true events. The re-creation of circumstances, locales, and conversations were derived from data including informational interviews, public records, newspaper and magazine articles, online information, state and local law enforcement records, and court documents. Names were changed to protect the anonymity of individuals and to support the assault victims' right to privacy. Some identifying characteristics and details such as physical properties, occupations, and places of residence were also altered.

ACKNOWLEDGEMENTS

I will always be grateful to my family and friends who believed in my endeavor. To my husband, your knowledge, encouragement, and support made this journey possible.

Thank you to Amy Lorenti, my book cover and layout designer, Tracy Kaminer, the editor of my copy, and the numerous readers who offered suggestions for further clarity of the story. You each understood and helped me to deliver the message. Without you, this book would have never been published.

Lastly, a special acknowledgement goes to the police men and women, first responders, EMS technicians, detectives, firearms instructors, police chaplain, and medical personal whose professionalism and expertise helped this woman make sense of and survive her experience.

CONTENTS

ARMED SURVIVOR

CHRISTINE GONZALES

Introduction

An honorable citizen, a disturbed criminal, and a lifelong addiction to violence, control, and sexual abuse, were on the agenda. *ARMED SURVIVOR* is the true account of two lives on a horrific collision course. The story is filled with twists and turns, intrigue and suspense.

Violence against women has reached epic proportions in the United States. In this case, a veteran school counselor and single woman appeared to take all the right precautions to live alone "safely." Smart, aware, and responsible, this independent lady possesses the survivor's instinct, but did she have what it would take to battle this demon?

Unbeknownst to her, this stalker watched from a distance. He tracked her every move, day and night, weekdays and weekends for several months. Lurking in the dark, this predator, a Cuban national, planned his attack. Had he done this before? Was he seeking asylum in the United States to avoid jail time in Cuba for pending rape and murder charges?

Was the United States to become his sanctuary from punishment for crimes committed? It will become apparent that this convicted felon and pathological liar did not fear extradition, our legal system, the U.S. Immigration and Customs Enforcement agency, or the Department of Homeland Security.

Follow these two lives to understand how this freak encounter between two strangers occurred; then, learn how to protect yourself from such attacks.

Travel Timeline

THE COUNSELOR

2008 - Spring, South Carolina

2008 - Duluth, Georgia

2008 - Norcross, Georgia

2009 - Spring, South Carolina

2009 - Lawrenceville, Georgia

2010-2011 - Duluth, Georgia

ISRAEL PEREZ PUENTES, CUBAN NATIONAL

2008 - Laredo, Texas

2009 - Grand Island, Nebraska

2010 - Alpharetta, Georgia

2011 - Duluth, Georgia

Two Lives, Two Paths, One Interaction

CHAPTER 1
Home on the Range

Spring, South Carolina
April 2008

Bang! Pop! Bang! "Hold your fire!" Faster than the speed of sound, bullets spiraled through the air. Suddenly all movement came to a halt.

"Place your guns down on the table. Don't touch the ammunition," the man demanded. "Clear your firearm, set the slide back, and step away from your pistols."

A few moments passed, and the man yelled, "We're cold! We're cold!" He sauntered up and down the line and called out instructions. "If you just arrived, it's time to set up your targets; everyone else, keep your hands off your weapons."

With only a staple gun in hand, Jim centered several targets on the wooden frame covered with corrugated cardboard that was set 25 feet from the table. My fiancé would be my instructor for the day.

Uncomfortable, I stood with my hands in my pockets staring down at my shoes that were covered with dust from a mixture of red clay and sand. It was a beautiful day in April of 2008; warm temperatures, perfectly clear, calm winds: a ten on any weatherman's scale.

Was I really about to do this? No one in my family ever owned a gun of any kind, pistol, rifle, or shotgun. Growing up in Connecticut, we spent time enjoying the beach during the summer and mountains during the winter. Snow and water skiing, fishing, sailing, ice-skating, and hockey were just a few of the activities I reveled in when I was not exploring the woods that surrounded our childhood home.

The four of us were very athletic and enjoyed taking on challenges. Only two members of my family ever spent time in the military, so they were the ones familiar with shooting pistols and rifles. Soon, it would be my time. I stared ahead at the targets.

To my left and my right stood men of all ages, from teens to retirees; each chatted about events of the past week.

Suddenly the man dressed in the fluorescent orange vest shouted, "Ears on! Eyes on! We're hot! We're hot!"

I understood the rules, which included wearing hearing and vision protection while at the pistol and rifle ranges. Other times I had visited Granchester State Forest Shooting Range, I was there to watch and observe the sharp shooters; today would be different.

Dating a military man from South Carolina meant I was going to learn more about weapons, handguns on this particular day. Would I be too scared to handle one safely? Could I hit the target? I prayed nothing would go wrong. Listening to directions was my main focus.

On the wooden table in front of me was a display of pistols, including a .22 caliber

Browning Buckmark, made for target practice, and a 9MM Glock Model 26. Jim handed me the clip and the bullets for the .22.

"You're ready to load," Jim instructed. He took this business seriously. A decorated retired Lieutenant Colonel of the United States Air Force who had earned a Distinguished Flying Cross, Jim Arthur could be trusted. After 24 years of manning a ship, this F-16 pilot knew the devil was in the details.

When he spoke, I listened. I inserted each bullet carefully, sliding them into place.

"Only three to start," he stated; we were practicing after all.

Next step, how to handle the pistol; where to place the hand and fingers on the gun. Then we reviewed the shooting stance necessary for accuracy, speed, and safety.

"Ready?" he asked.

I nodded in acknowledgement, focused my vision through the front and back sites, and then refocused my eyes on the target ahead of me.

"Lean into, not away from the target. Keep your weight forward and allow some bend to your knees. You want to provide stability and have your weight evenly distributed," Jim directed.

It was time. I pulled the trigger, and the gun fired; one, two, three. To my surprise, they all hit the target.

"Your main focus should be to get them in the target area. Don't worry about hitting a bull's-eye for now. If you ever need to use a weapon in a real life and death situation, you would aim at the target, and fire until you empty the magazine."

"Got it." I noticed the gun barrel remained open when all the bullets had been fired. We continued to practice until the casings from the 50 rounds of ammunition scattered about our feet.

It was time to make the switch and step-up the experience. Jim reached for the Glock. The 9MM bullets were larger in size and would do more damage to the target.

"You'll need to hold the grip tight," he commented. "You will feel a stronger kick from the recoil of the 9MM bullets." Once again shots rang out…one, two, and three. An encore performance; each bullet hit the target.

"Ears off, eyes off, range is cold," the range officer shouted.

It had been a successful morning. We packed up our belongings and exited the grounds.

While driving back to Georgia, I had time to think. I wondered why there were no other women shooting at the pistol range?

As time passed and my visits became more frequent to South Carolina, I did indeed meet women, who, like me, were hoping to gain confidence in the safe use of weapons for target practice. I was not alone in my curiosity.

CHAPTER 2
First Alert

Duluth, Georgia
May 2008

I opened my eyes and total blackness surrounded me. I was startled by a sound. Basically blind since birth, I scrambled to reach for my glasses. Was I dreaming? The doorbell rang again. I turned to the clock and saw the time glowing 2:35 a.m. on the digital display. Then, there was a knock at the front door. Keeping the lights off, I slowly made my way down the hallway into the living room. Peering through the mini blinds, I saw a police officer in uniform and the lights flashing from multiple police cars on the street in front of my home. I cracked the door open slowly.

"I want to alert you that we are searching your backyard for a suspect. Your property is not fenced in, and we have reason to believe he may be hiding there. Do not be alarmed," the policeman said.

"Okay, thank you." I closed the door slowly and turned the deadbolt to the locked position. My heart was still pounding.

Figures in the dark scattered across the surface of the lawn behind the house. My eyes followed the dancing dots of flashlight beams as they floated across the ground.

Chatter continued between the officers when a security light sensor popped the spotlight on across the street. Suddenly the neighborhood dogs began to bark. It was then I saw two figures emerge from the darkness into the illumination of flickering blue strobe lights. The police had done it! They apprehended the criminal. The perpetrator was escorted to the squad car in handcuffs. After being placed in the backseat, the group of men exchanged a few more words and retreated to their respective vehicles. Soon the police dispersed from the scene. Yes, I thought. I could sleep peacefully once again; no worries.

The next day I shared my experience with several of my friends at work.

"Do you have an alarm system?" Sara asked.

"No, I always felt safe in my home."

"Get a dog," another suggested playfully. I knew that would not be an option with Catnip, my Russian Blue feline; he would not tolerate that at all.

During lunch, Diane pulled me aside. "Do you have a minute to chat?" she inquired. She was soft spoken, loved by her students, and a top-notch math teacher. She was slight in build and stood just five feet tall. Her energy was amazing; this trait kept her students on task. Methodical by nature, she was an excellent instructor. These characteristics would be important for any firearms owner. Diane's home was located a few miles from mine in Duluth and she, too, lived alone.

"Do you own a gun?" she asked.

"No, do you?" I asked. I was caught off guard by her question and even more shocked by her answer.

"Yes. I have a .38 revolver. My friend owns a gun store in Decatur, and I purchased it for home protection. You can always ask him questions if you are interested in buying one."

I appreciated her offer and placed this suggestion in my vault of a brain. How many other women owned weapons? This question led me to continue my impromptu survey, and what I heard astonished me. Several more of my lady friends indeed owned handguns; a .357 magnum, a .22 caliber, and a 9MM Glock Model 27. With each person I approached, the number of women I knew who owned handguns was on the rise.

Now my mind was spinning. Over the past year, I had practiced with a firearm during my visits to South Carolina, but I had never thought about doing the same in Georgia. In addition, what about using a weapon for self-protection? This was a question I was about to contemplate this day in May of 2008.

CHAPTER 3
It's a "Sign"

Norcross, Georgia
June 2008

As I drove to work along Peachtree Industrial towards Atlanta, I noticed a neon sign above a single story building. An indoor gun range was located just a mile from my home, and I had never noticed it. Norcross Gun Club and Range was scrolled across the building in red, white, and blue lights easily seen from the car at 6:45 a.m. I felt this was more than a sign; it was a signal. At that moment, I knew I would need more information.

By 4 p.m. my workday at the private school was done. I counseled multiple students and their parents on the college planning process; now it was time to make my own plan.

I sped up the highway heading home to Duluth. After mulling over the idea all day, I had made my decision; I would stop by the range and inquire about their services.

Pulling in the parking space, I felt my nerves come to the surface. I anxiously exited the car and headed for the door. I had a feeling it would be all men inside and wondered if I would even be recognized as a customer of interest.

"Welcome," the man behind the counter said with a smile. "Can I help you?"

I smiled and walked towards the gentleman.

"Let me introduce myself. I'm Tom, an instructor on the premises." He seemed kind and approachable. We shook hands and I began my inquisition.

"Well, let me tell you a little bit about us," Tom said. "We do sell guns, we have several lanes in our indoor range for practice, and we offer instruction and training every day of the week. Matter-of-fact, there's a police officer here today from the Gwinnett County Police Department. She is offering tips on self-defense involving the use of a handgun for women. It is a free service we offer every Thursday."

What I didn't realize was that moment would change my life. The policewoman was available, and we began our brief but very important session.

"Have you ever handled a pistol?" she asked.

"Yes. I used a .22 caliber and 9MM at a range in South Carolina. My fiancé is in the military and he has started to work with me."

"Let's begin with a .22 then," the officer suggested.

This expert reviewed the fundamentals, which included how to hold the weapon, loading and inserting the clip, racking it, the stance, sight alignment, and trigger squeeze. We practiced picking it up quickly from a table and aiming the barrel at the mass on the target. She showed me how to securely place my elbows against my sides between my ribs and hips while gripping the firearm.

"This stance will allow you to hold the gun securely when you are in tight situations. If you extend your arms and hold the weapon out and away from your body, it could be pulled from your hands by your attacker," the officer pointed out.

This made perfect sense to me; a new tip for the day. I left the range considering the need for more practice sessions and contemplating my first purchase.

CHAPTER 4
The First Purchase

Lawrenceville, Georgia
June 2008

The decision to own a firearm would prove to be an important one. I wanted to become more proficient at handling a weapon while continuing to develop my skills during target practice; after all, I had enjoyed hitting the bull's eye. To make this happen, I would need to purchase a pistol of my own.

The Bass Pro Shop was located in Lawrenceville off highway 316. I entered the store and headed towards the game heads, deer mounts, and other exotic animals hanging high on the wall. Slowly, I browsed the glass counter where the guns were displayed. There were so many to choose from.

The salesperson introduced himself. "Welcome. My name is John. How can I help you today?"

I shook his hand and said, "I'd like to purchase a target pistol, a .22 caliber."

Strolling along the counter, I spotted a Browning Buckmark with the wood handle and a gold trigger. It was the same style as the one I used at the range, just a tad fancier in detail. "That's the one!" I indicated by pointing my finger to the third one from the left.

John reviewed all the features; how to load and unload the clip, what was needed to clean and care for it, a 500 round brick of .22 caliber ammunition for target practice as well as a box of Stingers, hollow-points, for home-defense. He explained a hollow-point bullet is an expanding bullet that has a pit or hollowed out shape in its tip often intended to cause the bullet to expand upon entering a target. A full metal jacket or target ammo are round-nosed bullets that tend to punch through the target and not deliver its energy into what's being hit.

"Next we have to complete an application and background check. Do you have your driver's license?" he asked.

"Yes, here you go," I said passing him the card.

"This process will take about 15 minutes to complete since I have to call the Georgia State Police and the national database."

Soon John returned and my paperwork was finalized. I was approved to pay for the firearm, my first purchase this day in June of 2008.

"If you ever have any questions, call or come back to our store," John said.

I assured him I would, and he escorted me out of the store with my items and off I went, home to examine my new purchase. This was exciting!

The next task was to obtain a concealed carry permit. It was important for me to have one in order to feel comfortable driving to and from the indoor range with my recent purchase. Research would continue online. The website revealed that Weapons Carry Licenses were issued in the Vital Records Division of the Probate Court in Gwinnett County. I recorded what was required: documents, data, and application. Fingerprinting would have to be done within five days of submitting the application and be taken to the Gwinnett County Permits Unit located at One Justice Way. Cost $77.50 total.

The Gwinnett County Courthouse was enormous. I had never been called to jury duty, so this was my first visit. One after another, the line of visitors moved through the x-ray machine. Ahead of me were signs pointing to the office for firearms permits. Before arriving to the site, I had reviewed the rules and regulations in regards to gun ownership, including legal issues, gun safety, and the numerous other responsibilities that come with being a proprietor and carrier. Once the paperwork was completed for Georgia's concealed carry license, I made my way to the next office for fingerprints. The permit would be sent to me by mail within the next 90 days. With this knowledge, I returned through the towering atrium and exited the courthouse feeling a sense of accomplishment and a new found sense of safety.

CHAPTER 5
The Land of the Free

Laredo, Texas
December 2008

According to the Border Patrol's report, five men set sail for seven days in a handcrafted boat from the island of Cuba to the coast of Mexico, landing their vessel in Cancun on December 6, 2008. Each man was seeking asylum.

The first leg of the journey was complete. The group spent seven days staying with a local fisherman in the area before making their way to a city where they could board a bus to Nuevo Laredo, Mexico. From there the five squeezed into a taxi and were dropped off at the foot of the International Bridge. They gathered what money they could pool together, paid the driver, and departed the vehicle. The men proceeded across the Gateway to the Americans, the pedestrian walkway, which led to the Port of Entry at Laredo, Texas.

The Border Patrol Agent at Bridge One arrested each member of the group. They took turns presenting their documents. The first in line was Israel Perez Puentes. He came from the Isla De La Juventud in Provincia de Ciudad de La Habana in Cotorro, Cuba, and advanced to the official staffing station of the United States Customs and Border Patrol Agency. He met with Officer CBPO Jose Luna. It was 8:00 a.m. when he was escorted to Hard Processing on December 26, 2008. Authorized personnel, CBPO Oscar Gonzalez conducted a Pat Down for Detention and Security purposes witnessed by CBPO Jose Luna and authorized by Supervisor Robert Daniels. It yielded a negative result. He was interviewed by Officer Oscar Gonzalez and read his rights and an I-214A form was executed for immigration/citizen status. The subject understood and signed the 1-214A and was processed for the Notice to Appear Proceedings (NTA). Under a Sworn Statement, the applicant shared his reason for leaving Cuba witnessed by Officer Jose Luna. The others followed suit.

Next was the interview. Puentes stated his intentions, to claim Political Asylum.

"I don't want to go back to Cuba for political reasons."

He would not be more specific except to state he could not express his true feelings and opinions and had no freedoms in Cuba. It appeared his freedom had been taken away due to his conduct in his community. The key question for the agent to decide: was he seeking refuge to avoid jail time in his homeland? The agent continued asking his list of questions before he made a final assessment.

Puentes was processed for Notice to Appear (NTA) Removal Proceedings, and was paroled into the United States pending 240 Removal Proceedings. The subject was found to be inadmissible pursuant to section 212 (a)(7)(A)(i)(l) of the INA and was processed for NTA Proceedings. Paroling an individual meant he or she was free to leave the agency and stay with relatives or friends anywhere in the United States until his or her Master Hearing.

Once provided with the *List of Free Legal Services*, Puentes made a sworn statement. He, the subject, expressed fear of persecution upon being returned to Cuba. He would not address why he feared imprisonment. His name was queried through the National Crime Investigation Center (NCIC) of the Federal Bureau of Investigation, and Computer Information System (CIS), which produced negative results. The agent made notations; the documents appeared real.

The system of the Immigration and Customs Enforcement, also known as ICE, had begun the long, arduous process of paroling Puentes into the United States. Though he came into this country in December of 2008, his first Master Hearing would not be scheduled until February of 2010, almost two years later. He was assigned a defense attorney who was knowledgeable of the protocol and understood how a case could be delayed if need be.

Edinburg, Texas was 156 miles from Laredo; this was Puentes' next destination. Once released from holding, he would reside with his cousin for a week or two. He knew Cuba would never accept him back since there are no extradition treaties with the United States. It would be impossible to be deported to his country of origin and he was relying on this.

Soon, Puentes made contact with another uncle on his mother's side and continued his trek from Texas, across Louisiana, through Mississippi and Alabama, to Florida. He would share an apartment with Ricardo in Miami, Florida, for a short time. It would be his welcome to The Sunshine State. It was his temporary sanctuary.

Puentes' uncle made connections with a group in South Carolina. In Lyman, an owner of a peach orchard would be hiring and Ricardo would bring his family to the compound. He asked Puentes to join them but he stayed behind. A paper trail would reveal Puentes traveled from Miami to Hialeah, Florida, settling in one apartment after another while working at odd jobs.

The Cuban community was close-knit in Florida, and Puentes' contacts were growing in number. Each individual had his or her connections concerning job opportunities throughout the United States. Puentes would keep his ear to the ground. These acquaintances shared information regarding jobs for day laborers in Nebraska with each other. It would not be long before he found himself traveling north on Interstate 75, the main artery through the country, to the land of the corn huskers, otherwise known as The Beef State. He would continue to maintain an address in Florida for the next two years while he explored other opportunities.

CHAPTER 6
Practice Makes Perfect

Spring, South Carolina
February 2009

Years of practice were paying off. I became a frequent flyer at the indoor gun range in Georgia and the Granchester State Forest Shooting Range in South Carolina. My goal was to become proficient and comfortable handling a firearm while enjoying the sport of target practice.

Call it a woman's intuition or a gut feeling, but I had become more concerned with safety in my home since the police knocked on my door in the early morning hours looking for their fleeting suspect.

I had been doing some serious soul searching about my feelings in regards to self-protection and home-defense. I carried pepper spray in my car and to use while taking my daily walks. Did I need more? This self-evaluation led me to consider numerous questions that were tough to contemplate. Did I believe that there could ever be a circumstance that would make it acceptable to use a handgun to hurt another if it was in self-defense? Could I really take aim and pull the trigger if my life was threatened? Would I be able to live with the legal, emotional, social, and spiritual ramifications that could come from my choices?

I had to be sure. I knew I would defend my life, but by what means? These decisions could affect my relationships too, but this was a personal decision that I had to make.

Over time, my final decision became clear; I would own a firearm to defend my life.

As my practice continued, the next decision dealt with which type of home defense weapon would best suit my needs. Salespersons shared their different opinions. I researched Glocks, Smith & Wessons, Taurus, Springfields, F & Ns, and Kimbers online. Each gun manufacturer had models in different calibers. My military friends and girlfriends offered their thoughts, too. There was no way to know except to try them, and I knew just the person to help me with that conundrum.

I made the call. "I want to try shooting a variety of firearms. I purchased a target pistol like yours, but I want to buy one for home protection. Do you think you can help me, Jim?"

"Sure thing…next time you come over I'll gather up several pistols I think you may want to use for self-defense, home protection, and possibly for carrying. Then we'll head to the range and try them out."

"I knew I could count on you," I said. "I'll see you this weekend."

I arrived in town on Friday evening, and we made our plans to head to Granchester in the morning. Jim gathered a few handguns from his collection; I would indeed find my comfort zone, a firearm I felt confident owning and carrying. I tried them all. Each had its own feel, grip, weight, sight, and power.

On my way back to Atlanta, I stopped by my friend's gun shop in Decatur, Georgia to browse some more. Adoringly, I gazed at the Bond-style Walther PPK, but I could not make such a splurge at that time. I did, however, spot my next purchase, a Bersa Thunder .380. It was to be my second investment of the year.

By 2010, *Top Shot,* a show on the History Channel, caught the eye of a new viewer. It was a show about contestants that competed in various types of shooting challenges. One by one, the contestants are eliminated until only one would remain. This would indeed become a sport I would enjoy.

CHAPTER 7
Welcome to Grand Island

Grand Island, Nebraska
March 2009

JBC USA, a leading processor of quality beef products in the U.S. opened a state-of-the-art distribution center at the company's beef processing plant in Grand Island, Nebraska, in 2013. Jift & Co. had previously owned the site. "We are dedicated to providing the best possible service, selection, and value to our customers," the new owner reported.

The operation in Grand Island was established in 1965 and was located on 131 acres in central Nebraska. The facility employed more than 3,200 team members and had the capacity to process more than 5,400 head of cattle per day.

The plant had not been without its problems. In 2006, ICE coordinated and deported undocumented workers. The company had been investigated for ten months prior to the raid. Of the 1,297 arrested, approximately 240 individuals were ultimately charged with crimes (in addition to administrative immigration violations). About 65 were charged with identity theft. A follow-up study was completed in 2009 and revealed that the Jift & Co. plant was paying better wages because of the need to attract new workers.

Grand Island residents were reeling in chaos from the changes in the town. Growth had been stagnant until the wages were increased. Outsiders would come to live there any way they could. Some workers got the idea that working for the plant was a good deal, but ended up hating the work, and leaving town. The first to arrive were members of the Vietnamese community, followed by Laotians,

Bosnians, and Sudanese. The vast majority, were from Latin America, mostly Mexico.

There had been conflict between the company and the Somalian community in regards to the Somali's request for prayer and worship during work hours. This led to a departure of members from this particular group, resulting in a large vacancy that had to be filled swiftly. The company found replacements in Florida, and notified the public school system that it would receive an influx of children from Cuban refugees. There was a 70 percent turnover in employees.

Residents of the community were ambivalent. They would exchange thoughts on these questions: Would the turmoil of the constant turnover ease the anger over unfair wages and the change in the population? Could the international community and longtime residents live more peacefully with the company's new strategy? Could Jift & Co. operate more efficiently and profitably if it responded to its chronic labor crisis by investing in a plan that would improve wages and working conditions at the plant? Would this plan prove to be beneficial in recruiting new workers?

Puentes was about to find out what life was all about in Grand Island first hand. He landed a job as a day laborer at Jift & Co when he arrived in town in March of 2009. He also found his first apartment on the main drag in this city of 46,000 residents.

CHAPTER 8
A Predator Strikes

Grand Island, Nebraska
June 2009

Everyone and everything was new. Puentes began this next stage of life surveying his surroundings. He scanned the town for the hangouts. The nightlife was not as lively as Florida, but he would make his own fun. It was easy to walk to most restaurants, businesses, and malls in the area. He had his uncle's car, too. He had the means to get to and from work. He would not need to depend on anyone for transportation.

It was not long before Puentes found himself watching the people of Grand Island.

While he surveyed the town, he spotted someone intriguing. A young woman, Danita Hernandez, was small in stature with a friendly smile. She caught the eye of a newcomer who lived only a few miles from her. She went about her business, working and enjoying life in her town. Danita spoke Spanish, which would make it easy for Puentes to communicate, and her appearance and dress reminded him of home. What she did not know was that she would become his focus.

According to reports, Puentes followed her around town. He trailed her to work and observed her schedule during the week and on the weekend. Soon he would have a record of her every move. He stalked her. She had no idea there were eyes on her.

It was 3:30 p.m. on Saturday, June 20, 2009, when Danita returned home from completing her errands. She noticed a man walking up her driveway. He slowly moved towards her door. She felt uncomfortable with the look in his eye, so she made a quick decision to call 911. Danita reported that someone had followed her to her apartment, and gave the police her address, sharing her fear.

The next thing Danita observed was the man covered in tattoos walking along side of her car. He kicked the car and used his fist to pound the windshield. He continued up the drive and forcefully entered her home without her permission.

"Get out! The police are on their way," Danita shouted in Spanish.

Puentes did not respond; he would not leave. He made movements towards her, grabbing her. He threatened to rape her, to kill her. Within a minute, the Grand Island police arrived on the scene. They made their way into the premises through the unlocked door and ordered the predator to release her. He resisted at first, then was quickly subdued and placed in handcuffs.

The police watched as Puentes continued his rant toward Danita in their presence. He was not making any sense. He was escorted out of her home and brought to jail. The processing began for this new inmate. Within days, he came before a judge and was released on bond and assigned an attorney. He would receive a misdemeanor and a warning by the judge. This was a slap on the wrist to Puentes, and his first brush with the law in Grand Island.

Two days after the initial incident, June 22, Puentes appeared at Danita's place of employment. She caught a glimpse of him outside the window and went to her boss. She told him of her experience over the weekend, and they agreed to contact the police again.

Puentes heard the sirens approaching and calmly walked back to his car and exited the lot.

This young woman lived in fear. Danita would call the police two more times. "I am worried he will kill me," she said. "He came to me at work and threatened to fight after work. I have talked to my employers about the problem. I am afraid for my life." This man terrorized her. The police recommended that she complete a restraining order to protect herself from this stranger.

Another two days passed and Danita entered her request for a restraining order. It was June 24, 2009. She was asking for a protection order prohibiting the respondent, Puentes, from imposing any restraint upon her or upon her liberty; prohibiting the respondent from harassing, threatening, assaulting, molesting, or attacking her or otherwise disturbing her peace; and prohibiting the Puentes would keep his distance. She wondered why he was following her. She had never met him; she did not know him. Details of these events were noted in the court documents.

CHAPTER 9
Eviction

Grand Island, Nebraska
July 2009

Puentes had been in Grand Island since March of 2009. He did not have respect for people or places. Though he was employed, he was not paying his bills including his rent. Before long, he would be served an eviction notice on July 8 of the same year. The notice to vacate the premise demanded he remove himself and his belongings within three days of the termination of rental agreement. Puentes was to appear in Civil Court in Hall County, Nebraska to face the plaintiff, J & B Rentals, the owner of the rental unit.

A Petition for Restitution of Premises was filed by the owner of the complex on July 14. The Writ of Restitution was to remove the Defendant, Puentes, from the possession of the premises and for judgment against the Defendant for the following: Declaring the parties' lease agreement forfeited and terminated; awarding possession of the described premises to the Plaintiff; for $620.00 for the rent and late fees now due and owing and unpaid and for such further sums as may accrue between the filing of the complaint and the rendition of judgment; for reasonable attorney's fees as provided by the Nebraska courts together with the cost of this action; and for such other and further relief as the Court may deem Plaintiff entitled.

It was Puentes second time in court. He was assigned an attorney who he agreed to pay for services rendered once the case closed. He appeared in the courtroom and faced the plaintiff. The judge heard the case and found in favor of the J&B Rentals. Puentes was ordered to pay restitution and court fees. He would pay for the rental, but he claimed he would need to repay the attorney when he had earned enough funds.

The search was on for a new apartment. Within a few days, Puentes had a new address, 709 W. Louisa St. in Grand Island, which was off the main drive. Again, everything he would need was within walking distance. This rental was not too far from a local restaurant and a short drive to work. He would watch the locals: where they shopped, where they pumped gas, and where public transit picked up and dropped off passengers.

Meanwhile, a hardworking mother of four, Sandi Tolmen, would exchange glances with the man with four tattoos while working at her two jobs: one, at a clothing shop at the mall and the other, at a local eatery called Ruby Tuesday.

CHAPTER 10
Multiple Attacks

Grand Island, Nebraska
August 2009

Several weeks had passed, and Puentes was getting used to his new apartment. He had also found a new obsession. Puentes would trail Sandi to work and home. When he was not at Jift & Co., he walked a mile to her home. He watched her children play in the yard and noted friends coming and going from her home. He would follow her many times before finding the right moment to make his introduction.

Sandi was finishing her shift at one job and headed home in the afternoon for a quick nap. She needed some rest and her children would be out of the house for a while. She pulled into the driveway, put the car in park, grabbed her purse and keys, and headed for the front door. What she did not notice was that someone was tailing her; it was the same person who had followed her home many times before, unbeknownst to her.

The cycle was about to start over. The timing turned out to be perfect and little did she know Puentes would become a threat.

Sandi placed her belongings on the table and made her way to her living room where she lay down on her couch to catch a few minutes of peace and relaxation. She dozed off.

This Monday, August 17, Puentes made his way into Sandi's home while she slept. He did not have permission to be there. He woke her up by slapping her. She was stunned and sat up motionless and speechless. He abruptly turned and went into her kitchen, got a knife, returned, and began swinging it in her direction. She tried to run, but he tripped her and she fell. Puentes got on top of her holding the knife to her throat. At that moment, a friend walked in. Puentes stood up and ran out the door.

What had just happened Sandi wondered. She was trying to process the experience and explain it to her ally. He promised to stay with her and protect her and her family when they returned home from school. She would also call the police to make a report.

Before long, Puentes was picked up by the police. He was charged with Terroristic Threats for threatening to kill Sandi with a knife. He would make bond and be out until the hearing.

Puentes was furious. He could not touch Sandi, but he it appeared he needed to take his anger out on someone.

Just three days after this event at Sandi's home, Puentes disregarded the restraining order Danita filed, and he arrived at her doorstep. Luckily, on August 20, Danita was alert and vigilant. She recognized the figure approaching her doorway and called the police immediately. Puentes had barged through her door and threatened to kill her again. Within minutes, the patrol officers arrived on the scene; they restrained him once more.

Puentes was immediately charged with threatening to commit a crime of violence with the intent to terrorize another person with reckless disregard and risk of causing terror. He would have two charges pending. He was taken to jail and was held until his hearing date, October 13, 2009.

While imprisoned, Puentes tried several tactics to gain release from the Grand Island facility according to the police files. He complained of respiratory issues and was placed on suicide watch the day he was admitted.

Initially this predator pled not guilty and was held over in the Hall County Department of Corrections. On October 27, he changed his plea to guilty and was given credit for 67 days served, and a plea bargain. Guilty by conviction, Puentes was to pay for the cost of his action with the court, and he was released. He had earned two felonies for Terroristic Threats and a new title, "convicted felon."

Had the courts made their report to ICE? Grand Island courts seemed to be lenient in their decision-making process. Had this happened before with other immigrants? Were they turning a blind eye because of their need for workers?

The city of Grand Island in Hall County was on the "Sanctuary Cities" list. "Sanctuary cities" protect criminal aliens from deportation by refusing to comply with ICE detainers or otherwise impede open communication and information exchanges between their employees or officers and federal immigration agents.

Residents of Grand Island, especially the women, lived in fear of Puentes' actions each day of the year. He would be allowed to continue his reign of terror. He was relentless.

CHAPTER 11
Another Protective Order

Grand Island, Nebraska
October 2009

S andi had counted the days until Puentes was released. Reports indicated she had been told by the county attorney, before his release on the charge of Terroristic Threats and the plea bargain, that he was going to be deported. She would be able to breathe a sigh of relief. Unbeknownst to her, he was not detained or deported by ICE.

Puentes did not forget about Sandi while he had been incarcerated. He spent his time focusing on how he would reconnect. Once released, he would immediately drive by

Sandi's house and stop by her place of employment on a daily basis. On October 26th and 27^{th,} he called her home and threatened to kill her. He proceeded to sit and wait for her children outside of their school. Sandi felt helpless once again. She made another report. She felt that the legal system had failed her.

Sandi recounted to the police that she lived in fear for her life and the lives of her children. Just ten days later, on November 4, Puentes came to her house wanting to talk to her. She again contacted the police to report the interaction.

"I told him 'no, I don't want to talk to you' and asked him to leave. Approximately an hour later while I was on my way to work, I received a phone message from a friend who was scared for me. He had stopped by my house to be sure I was okay when he saw Puentes' car in the driveway. I had left my home unlocked for my children, so my friend walked in through the front door. He searched each room and found Puentes just sitting on my bed in my bedroom. He told him to leave and he did," she recalled.

Puentes came back to her house the next day and threatened her and her friend once again. Sandi would have to take action.

On November 13, 2009, Sandi filed a Petition and Affidavit to Obtain a Domestic Abuse Protective Order with the Clerk of the District Court of the State of Nebraska to protect her and her children from this predator. She recorded all incidents in writing on her request form, including the verbal threats immediately after his release, his harassing phone calls, his stalking actions outside her place of employment, his waiting and watching for her children outside of the school they attended, and the appearance of this felon in her own bedroom.

Lastly, Sandi added, "On November 5, I was asleep upstairs in my bedroom when Puentes came into my home. I awoke to him standing at my door shaking, looking 'crazy' with his hand behind his back telling me to 'come with him, come with him.' I responded with, 'I'm not going with you, why are you in my house?' My friend woke up at that time and Puentes turned and ran out the back door leaving the knife he had held behind his back, on the kitchen counter. I was terrified and I told my friend he could have stabbed us both while we were sleeping."

Sandi put the details of the events in writing and begged the court to provide her with a protective order against Puentes for the safety and well-being of her and her children. She wrote, "I am afraid he is going to kill me if this pursues. I am scared for the safety of my children." She was angry and she was frightened. Her report was filed with the courts.

The Grand Island police kept an eye on his movements. Puentes had become a repeat offender in their Hall County court system.

CHAPTER 12
Misdemeanors

Grand Island, Nebraska
November 2009

People in the town of Grand Island, Nebraska were becoming all too familiar with Puentes. Once again, trouble was not far behind for this man. Terroristic Threats would not be his only charges for the month of November.

Mr. Jon Placke filed an application to the State of Nebraska vs. Israel Perez Puentes for the attorney's fees accrued on November 12. On April 1, 2009, this attorney was appointed to represent the defendant, Puentes, in a case that had reached its conclusion regarding an eviction notice. The attorney had not received payment for services and had no contract for the payment of any compensation from Puentes.

Later in November, Puentes was charged with credit card fraud by the owner of a stolen card. He received a misdemeanor when he could have been charged with another felony. No time was served; he paid restitution.

Puentes, a Cuban national, had violated at least two citizens of the United States since his arrival, and had several felony convictions for Terroristic Threats and a growing list of misdemeanors.

Records indicated Puentes maintained an address in Hialeah, Florida, as well as Nebraska. The holidays came and went, and he was back in Grand Island to continue work at the meat packing plant.

Puentes' rap sheet was growing according to the Nebraska State Police. On February 4, 2010, he was pulled over for a traffic stop and served a warrant by Lexington Police in Sarpy County. The charges included unlawful turning or stopping which earned him a citation and fine. Four days later, he was charged as a fugitive from justice; "Alien Inadmissibility under Section 212;" failure to appear or comply; no operator's license; possession of Fictitious plates; and Failure to Appear. He was awarded two more misdemeanors and released. The city of Lexington in Sarpy County was considered a "sanctuary city."

This felon continued to disregard the laws. He was making a mockery of our legal system.

CHAPTER 13
Single and Alone

Duluth, Georgia
January 2010

Burglars had hit the area and the news stories about gangs moving out of Atlanta towards the suburbs continued to be aired. Several houses in my subdivision had been broken into while the inhabitants were away. These groups were heading up the Buford Highway corridor into the towns of Norcross and Duluth. Luckily, no one on my street had had to deal with such issues. Was that because several homeowners worked out of their homes? Maybe – maybe not. As these incidents moved closer to home, I felt my inner alarm sound off a sense of warning. As a single woman living alone, I needed to be sure my surroundings were safe. I would learn to secure my premises.

My daily work schedule kept me running from my humble abode to school and back again Monday through Friday. The hours of my daily grind were fairly consistent, often leaving the driveway before the sun came up and arriving home by sunset. Occasionally, I would stay later for an evening college planning program or end my week with a sprint out of town to South Carolina, resulting in a quick turn-around by Sunday afternoon.

With each trek, I made a conscious decision to run through my very own security checklist.

I did not have an alarm system, but I was now in possession of legal firearms that could be used for self-protection while at home. While away, I always made sure to have the petsitter stop by two times a day to feed Catnip. The petsitter was my extra set of eyes on the weekends I was away.

My first check always started with the outside. The lawn was maintained weekly to have that "lived in" look, and the shrubs were cut low so no one would hide behind them. Motion sensor lights were installed on the four corners and were checked for illumination periodically. Prickly plants, including hollies and yuccas under my bedroom windows, added an extra layer of protection. The walkways around the sides and the back of my house were made of pea stone. This would serve as noise detection and early notification if unwanted visitors crunched as they crept along the paths.

An extra level of window locks had been added to each window frame. This added adjustment should help if a burglar jimmied a pane. The additional attached lock would serve as a secondary level of assurance beyond the usual window lock. Each window had blinds for privacy, which were particularly important in the evenings and while away.

The solid wood front door was set with a deadbolt lock and a regular lock and key inset for the doorknob. An enormous Christmas bell ornament, the size of an orange, was placed on the handle of the interior garage door. It could provide an early notification of entry should

58 – Single and Alone

someone open the door from the garage. The doorknob had an interior lock on it as well.

My main problem was the sliding glass door. I read that one could place a stick or dowel on the track on the inside of the stationary frame and that would prevent the door from sliding open. This was not an option for me due to an installation issue. The door had been set in the frame in reverse position when the house was built. It did have a levered lock handle; however, that latch was not the most secure option for locking either. A friend offered a very smart suggestion, which was to drill a hole in the bottom of the doorframe so a long pin could be installed. The pin would connect through the two steel frames when the door was closed making the stationary glass door and the sliding glass impossible to open. This seemed like a fantastic option; it seemed secure, or so I thought.

The backyard boundaries bordered four homes, and there was another house directly across the street. Each home was inhabited. Two of the households had dogs that were vigilant at letting us know if someone was around the premises.

The trash was always removed, never leaving boxes at the edge of the driveway indicating newly purchased items. My neighbors picked up my mail, and I stopped the delivery of the paper when I was away. Timers were set on various lights and each would come on and go off at different times during the week, even when I was home. There was an agreement between neighbors that we would keep an eye out for each other's properties, a neighborhood watch of sorts.

Overall, I had a sense of confidence that if someone entered my house without my permission during the day while I was at home, I would certainly hear him or her. I would now defend myself with my weapon of choice. Before my purchases, I had kept a can of hornet spray ready that would shoot at least 14 feet in distance. It would be accurate for blinding someone from afar. Though I had a landline, my cell phone was kept within reach. At night, should a burglar enter while I slept, my handguns lay on the nightstand within reach.

Admittedly, it took some time to feel comfortable having a clip in the gun with the safety off. I was still getting use to the red dot…hot or not. There would be a learning curve.

My checklist was complete.

CHAPTER 14
The Marriage and Assault

Alpharetta, Georgia
February - August 2010

I t was time to make a change. Puentes had overstayed his welcome in Nebraska, but he also had a score to settle with the targets of his obsessions.

A new plan was being developed; Puentes needed to gain citizenship to the land of the free for good. How could he make this happen sooner rather than later? He sprang into motion; his next goal was to marry a citizen of the United States.

Two hearing dates with ICE had passed in early 2010 without Puentes' appearance. He had his defense attorney change venues that would delay the next hearing until September of 2010. He could not let the Immigration Office know of his felony and misdemeanor charges. He would have to make a change.

Puentes packed up his car and headed southeast leaving the views of the plains of Nebraska in his rearview mirror. He traveled through Kansas City, St. Louis, and Chattanooga towards Florida before exiting Interstate 75 in Atlanta. The Cuban community had a niche in the Atlanta area, in the northeast suburbs in particular. Norcross, Duluth, Roswell, Alpharetta, Cumming, and Johns Creek, were cities where he would find friendship and camaraderie. There was a large population of second and third generation Cuban Americans in these towns, many of who had relocated from South Florida. It is easier to blend into the communities if you live in a city versus a small town or rural area. This locale was close to his family in South Carolina, but far enough away to do whatever type of activity he wanted to pursue.

Construction jobs were plentiful in the area. Puentes would make this locale his new home. He had a budding social life and his acquaintance introduced him to his future wife Vanda.

Puentes and Vanda met and decided to tie-the-knot very quickly. By July of 2010, the newlyweds were celebrating their first month of marriage. They would reside in Alpharetta, Georgia, in Vanda's home in Fulton County. Stage one of his plan was complete, and she appeared to be on board. Timing indicated they would be married for as long as it would take the immigration process to reach completion.

Though Puentes had the appearance of settling down, his anger continued to get the best of him. He had a score to settle, and his obsession continued with several women in the Midwest even after he was married. Another trip to Grand Island, Nebraska was added to his schedule, and Puentes would find himself in trouble once more. Early in August 2010, a month after his wedding, Puentes was charged as a suspect in an assault case in Grand Island. The charges were suspiciously dropped for reasons unknown.

CHAPTER 15
Cutting A Deal

Alpharetta, Georgia
January 2011

Upon Puentes' return to Georgia, he continued to file the paperwork with the Immigration Office under a new alias; he had to. He had managed to obtain a long list of felonies and misdemeanors since he crossed the border just two years prior. He made a new decision; he would use only his first and middle name on his application. Perez was his mother's maiden name. The documents would read Israel Perez instead of Israel Perez Puentes.

This perpetrator of numerous crimes had yet to attend a hearing since he had been paroled into the United States in December of 2008. Puentes would hide this legal history from ICE while he applied for the employment authorization documents (EAD). There was a problem; he had not filed the I-485 form, the Application for Permanent Residence or Adjust Status as expected in February of 2010. It would take him another eight months to complete and file this form with the payment by September 2010. His file was sent to the San Antonio Case Control Office for review along with a filing with the Executive Office for Immigration Court.

For Puentes, this process was taking too long. The new year of 2011 brought many changes to the couple. He continued to keep in contact with the Department of Homeland Security. Form I-485 remained pending for review through April 2011, as was his I-765 form, the Application for Employment Authorization.

This felon was restless. What Puentes would do with this negative energy was anyone's guess. His past history would indicate he would go on the attack; he needed to make a move.

It took Puentes a week to find the right place to raid. He spent time driving in and out of subdivisions close to his Alpharetta home in Fulton County. He looked for dwellings that would make for an easy heist. Late one night in January, he hit the jackpot, a house vacated for the weekend in an established neighborhood.

A homeowner in the Cumming, Georgia neighborhood called 911 to report a suspicious individual in his neighbor's backyard. The couple observed what sounded like gutters being removed from a home whose unlucky residents were out of town. Several dogs in the subdivision started to bark, and they saw a man run from the premises in dark clothes to a vehicle that was parked in a nearby driveway. It backed out and sped down the street going southbound. The caller did not see the license plate.

Police arrived at the subdivision to check out the call. They spotted a car with out-of-state plates with an individual matching the description of the prowler exiting the only street out in the location. The officer turned his car around and followed the automobile. Promptly pulling over the vehicle, the officer ran the Florida plates and called for backup. A second police car pulled up to the scene. One officer approached the door and asked Puentes to get out of the vehicle slowly. He was dressed in a long sleeve black shirt, black gym pants, and black tennis shoes. He was out of breath since he had just run to his car. His hands were shaking.

The interview began with the first officer: "Where are you headed?"

At first, Puentes motioned he did not speak English. Finally, he responded, "I'm late for work."

"Where do you work?" the second policeman inquired.

Puentes refused to respond. Later he stated, "Down I-400 towards Abbotts Bridge." His appearance didn't jive with his story.

Another question was posed: "Where were you coming from?" Again, there was silence. Puentes could not justify his conduct.

The interrogation continued. "I will need your license." Puentes provided one of many.

"Are you in possession of any firearms?" the officer asked. He refused to respond.

The second patrolman began to search the interior of the car. Inside he found a 9MM Beretta handgun with a loaded clip shoved between the driver's seat and the center console. Also within reach were a set of dark grey gloves and a black ski mask. Then the officer requested that Puentes open the trunk of the 2007 Chrysler 300 Touring Sedan. Israel did. In the trunk, they located tools that could be used to break into a home, an LG flip cell phone, a black Sentry Safe, a Jesus statue, and ten dollars in currency wrapped in a towel. The handcuffs clicked around his wrists once more.

Puentes' last statement was, "The handgun belonged to a friend of mine." He was placed in the back of the police car.

The police transported him to Police Headquarters in Johns Creek where they ran a criminal history check. The officer noted in his report additional information. He wrote, "Israel Perez Puentes is a convicted felon out of the state of Nebraska for four counts of terroristic threats, and an additional four felony convictions, for unknown charges. In all, eight felony convictions were from the state of Nebraska."

Puentes was charged at that time with a felony possession of a firearm. According to the charge, the police then transported him to the Fulton County Jail. The 9MM Berretta semi-automatic pistol, magazine clip with fourteen 9MM rounds, black safe, black ski mask, gray gloves, LG phone flip phone, and tools for breaking into the house were entered into evidence. The Fulton County Court added the felony charge of commission of a crime while in possession of a firearm to the list. Other charges included loitering and prowling, and no tag light.

Puentes paced the floor of his cell. He would spend most of January in the Fulton County facility, which was a brief stay, compared to his time in Nebraska. His case came before the judge of the Fulton County Superior Court. His arrest record would read charges of loitering and prowling, possession of burglary tools in commission of a crime, and being a convicted felon in possession of a firearm. He was assigned a designated defense attorney who would represent him in his case. Puentes bonded out of jail and awaited trial.

The judge heard the lawyer's case and a plea bargain was agreed upon; Puentes struck another deal with the court. He, a known felon, would be released on a misdemeanor charge with the stipulation that he be placed on probation and never be in possession of a weapon again. Puentes had just received another slap on the wrist. He and his lawyer worked the system once more. The crime had been committed in a "sanctuary city."

Had the judge and the prosecuting attorney not found his previous record of arrests in Nebraska? Had they not run his name in the national database? Were the courts so overloaded that they did not feel the need to prosecute foreign nationals to the full extent of the law?

According to Nebraska State Police, Israel was a convicted felon, a multistate offender who was not allowed to purchase, own a gun, or be in possession of one. Having one in his control should have awarded him another felony charge resulting in jail time in Georgia.

The Federal Bureau of Investigation, the United States Department of Justice, and the Criminal Justice Services Division in Clarksburg, West Virginia, had a record of Puentes as a felon on charges of Terroristic Threats for which he served time in Nebraska. His fingerprints were in the system. He had the necessary papers to be detained according to his review at the border in December 2008.

With this encore performance before the judicial system, Puentes once again was free to terrorize and make a mockery of the legal system and immigration processing procedures while continung to endanger the lives of the citizens of the United States of America. To everyone who knew him and observed his behaviors, the final decision of probation did not make sense.

CHAPTER 16
A Touch of "the Nerves"

Duluth, Georgia
March 2011

As I retrieved my mail from the box at the end of the driveway, I noticed the garage door rise on my neighbor's house across the street and Johnny Fig stepped outside.

"What was Nala barking at last night?" I inquired of my neighbor in reference to the German shepherd's antics.

"I let her out if she hears something. Last night she chased a man strolling in front of our houses and down the street around midnight. He took off running," Johnny shared.

"Did you contact the police?" I inquired.

"No, he moved on pretty quick when he saw Nala. I doubt he'll be back. I saw him out the window, and I think he saw me."

I took note of his observation and made sure I took plenty of time to look around and inside my car before getting in and before exiting each day. While working in the yard, I kept the garage door closed and carried the keys to the front door. My cell phone was usually in my pocket. I noticed vehicles passing slowly by my house while I was out gardening. This was not so unusual, though. The neighborhood had plenty of children playing in the streets, and I was always glad when drivers were careful.

Again, the next night, I heard dogs barking into the wee hours of the morning and took this as another warning of something unusual happening outside my home. Maybe the dog was reacting to the sighting of a wild animal, a coyote perhaps.

For the third time, I was getting more nervous about my neighborhood. Three years had passed since my first handgun lesson, and I began to think about possibly carrying a weapon in my purse. My research led me to investigate a hammerless revolver. It seemed I would be less likely to accidently discharge a handgun in my handbag if it did not have a hammer to catch on edges. I felt more comfortable loading the bullets into the barrel than a clip, too.

I arrived at the indoor gun range in time to get some information from Tom.

"Welcome! It's good to see you back at the range. How can we help you today?" he asked.

"I am interested in learning more about revolvers since I think I may want to carry one. I have researched several models, but I thought I might be able to try some here for fit."

Tom suggested a Smith & Wesson Bodyguard, a .38 caliber revolver. I tried it out and it fit my hand well. It was light in weight. I was indeed more confident loading and unloading it.

"The trigger pull is a little longer than I am used to, but I love the red laser sight!" I shared after taking a few shots.

Tom reviewed gun safety, cleaning procedures, safe storage, secondary dangers, and so forth. The third sale was complete in March of 2011.

CHAPTER 17
From One Cell to the Next

Grand Island, Nebraska and
Alpharetta, Georgia
March - May 2011

B y March of 2011, Puentes found himself pacing the floor of his next cinderblock cell, only this time he was back in the Midwest. He could not let go of those he stalked. As luck would have it, Puentes heard the click of the key, the cell door opened, and he walked free through the revolving door once more. No further constraints, no added worries. He was like Houdini, making the charges disappear again. He beat the system. The traffic stop without a registration was only a minor setback. He paid the fine and was on his way. Puentes was free to continue to plot, to control, to terrorize, and to cause pain to his next target.

With this unsuccessful attempt in Nebraska to interact with his intended targets, Puentes would return to Georgia. Though agitated at this inconvenience, he already had his eye on a new mark.

The couple's relationship was short lived. Vanda filed for a separation in April of 2011 as planned and decisions about a divorce were looming in the near future. It had been eleven months since their wedding day and Puentes had been in and out of jail several times, racking up more felony and misdemeanor charges along the way.

So, where would Puentes live next now that he was newly separated? Who did he know in the area that would take him in? He had filed a permanent residence form for Georgia through the Immigration Office, but his only option was to look into South Carolina.

On May 2, Puentes would make a move. Lyman, South Carolina is located in the county of Spartanburg, 141 miles from Alpharetta,

Georgia. It was there that Puentes made contact with several relatives, including an uncle and cousins, who moved there from Cuba. His new home would be a sparse room on the uncle's compound in this peach orchard community. He found refuge there; it would be his home for the moment. Though he registered with the Immigration Office as residing in Georgia, he was now living in the Palmetto State.

Would these lies catch up with Puentes? The United States would not deport him according to Cuba's rules on extradition. His hope was that the change in name on the application would throw the Office of Immigration off track. Applications to Homeland Security continued to be reviewed at a snail's pace. Did Puentes know that his track record of felonies would affect his application for citizenship?

The divorce petition was to be set in motion and would be submitted on May 9, 2011. He thought his plans were on schedule for gaining citizenship, so there was no need to remain married.

Puentes' ride from Lyman to Alpharetta was now an hour and a half in length. He continued to travel down interstate 85 back to Georgia using a new mode of transportation: his uncle's car, a white Honda.

The next appointment to gain a Permanent Resident Card/Resident Alien Card was scheduled for May 11, 2011 in Atlanta. Puentes updated his address with the U.S. Citizenship and Immigration Offices continuing to use Vanda's Alpharetta address, even though he had moved to South Carolina.

The next hurdle for Puentes would be answering questions about his acts of terrorism in America including his felony convictions and other criminal acts. Soon ICE and The Department of Homeland Security would make a more permanent decision on his admission to our country as a citizen.

CHAPTER 18
The Chosen One

Duluth, Georgia
February - May 2011

Stalkers are obsessed with their targets by nature. Puentes always planned his actions in intricate detail. A loner, what he was doing was very important to him. He would induce fear and control over his victims. It was becoming apparent that Puentes was a born predator. It was about sexual gratification, control, and violence. He had his routine, as proven by the records of his attacks in Nebraska.

Puentes found his victims in various places doing every day activities: innocently shopping at a supermarket, pumping gas at a local filling station, window-shopping at the mall, eating at a restaurant, or just walking about the neighborhood getting some physical fitness.

Most of the time, Puentes' stalking behavior began as one of his relationships was ending. This time, he had been married, but it was a month away from becoming null and void. It had been short-lived, which was according to his plan. It appeared Puentes' married for one reason: the convenience and ease of gaining U.S. citizenship.

In the aftermath of this union, Puentes turned to his next obsession, his next chosen one.

Psychologists and other professionals working with sexual predators have noted the phases of attachments in their research: the attraction phase; the anxious phase, when the controlling behaviors show themselves; the obsessive phase, where stalking takes place, and the destructive phase. Israel was about to begin the process all over again.

Unbeknownst to anyone, the stalking ritual had begun in February of 2011. It would last on and off for three months. This time Puentes did not know his target. He had not spoken to her. She stood 5'7" tall, fair skin, blonde hair with an athletic build. His victim would not know she was being stalked. This predator planned his attack and rehearsed it as his sexual fantasies developed.

Frequent visits to the Berkeley Lake neighborhood continued over time, on weekdays and weekends. Puentes checked the entrance routes and the exits to the subdivision. He parked the car and walked the streets to get a lay of the land. This was done during the day and at night. Inhabitants of this subdivision, would come and go from their homes, conducting their daily routines oblivious to his new focus. He would take note. What time did the lights come on? Who had security systems and security lights? Who had dogs? Did more than one person live in the home? Did anyone remain home throughout the day? Was the yard fenced in?

Puentes often heard a neighbor's dog barking, which always caught his attention. He moved closer to observe more details of one particular home. He noticed there was no fence around the house, which would allow him to move closer. One floor, five windows, two doors, a garage, no alarm or signs anywhere, several motion detector lights, and a screened porch. Backyard shrubbery was used as a fence, good for hiding from the eyes of the neighbors. While the owner was at work, he peered in the windows to note where the bedrooms and baths were located. He did so undetected by anyone. In the early morning and late at night, he would sit in wait to watch the timed lighting schedule.

Countless hours were spent scouting out the area to fine tune his approach in the dark. Puentes watched for several weeks taking notes on his target's daily order of business. He noticed the movement in the house; around 5:30 a.m., the TV set lights would flicker through the blinds. By 5:45 a.m., the bathroom light would go on. He logged the progression of movement from the bedroom to the kitchen, the opening and closing of the porch door for the cat, lights being turned off in bathroom, bedroom, and kitchen, then out the door by

6:45 a.m. for work. Puentes made one more critical observation; the neighbors would wait to let their dogs out at 7:00 a.m. He headed back to the car before daylight only to return to confirm activities again and again.

The stalker was looking for his perfect window of opportunity. It was about to be a freak collision of lives.

CHAPTER 19
Like Clockwork

Duluth, Georgia
May 2011

My schedule ran like clockwork. It always had. After 30 years of working in a school and coping with Atlanta inbound traffic, I knew I never had time to spare. My alarm sounded promptly at the same time every day. I had my patterns. I turned on the television to watch the news and weather, would debate what to wear, pet the cat, then proceed to get ready for my day. In my head, I reviewed my work schedule while I made the bed, tossed on the throw pillows, and flipped the light switches in each room. The cat always loved a bit of fresh air in the morning so the door would open and close like clockwork. Catnips' bowl was filled with the delicacy for the day, and I was off to the shower. Dressed with makeup applied, hair dried, and decorative details added to my outfit for a pop of color, I was out the door. It often felt like I was a participant in Bill Murray's movie, *Ground Hog Day*.

There were the weekly runs to Publix for food, QuikTrip to fill-up the car, Home Depot for home repair items, Super Walmart for miscellaneous items, and dinner out with friends at local restaurants. Otherwise, each day was the same until it came to the weekend.

This particular weekend in May, my fiancé was coming to visit. Something felt different. I had a burning request for Jim to make the handgun safety feature "hot" or active on all three firearms.

"Please be sure the three are in the 'on' position so they are ready to fire. I'm not sure why," I requested.

"You're all set!" Jim said. We went about our weekend activities and he headed back to South Carolina that Sunday morning.

CHAPTER 20
Spotted

Duluth, Georgia
May 2011

Puentes continued to ride by the home of his intended target as he scanned the traffic patterns in the neighborhood this particular weekend in May. He was becoming more anxious and increasing sloppy with his tactics.

By Sunday, Puentes' actions caused several slip-ups. Spotted behind a tree at 3 a.m. by a resident who lived across the street from the intended victim, he, dressed in all black, sprinted to his waiting car as Nala, the German shepherd, took chase. This was the second time he had been sighted. Again, the neighbor did not call the police.

Neil Jones, a resident who lived down the street, saw a white car parked in front of the vacant lot over the weekend and thought the neighbors must have visitors in from South Carolina again.

While out in her garage, Rebecca Wisecoff, the neighbor who lived to right of the target's home, saw a white car parked on the street not far from my driveway on Monday morning. Once Puentes was observed, he backed the car up into a driveway and left the subdivision. It must be another visitor to the area, she thought. The next visual of the white car a few hours later gave her concern. The driver quickly made a three-point turn to reverse direction of the car on the street. The white car sped out of view.

The following day, Rebecca noticed what seemed to be the same car, slowly passing by her house. She did not write down the license plate, but took note that it looked like a four-door white Camry.

No one spoke to each other about what they saw. No reports were made to the police.

The scheduled date for Puentes' deadline was coming. He had an appointment to get his fingerprints taken in Atlanta on Wednesday, May 11. He asked his cousin if he could borrow her car once again, even though his license from Georgia had expired.

Just in case Puentes was stopped along the I-85 corridor, he made sure to have paperwork to present to an officer. There was an abundance of documents to choose from, including four licenses from various states under four different names, several applications for citizenship to the United States also under two distinct identities, two immigration IDs with two unique sets of numbers, and two social security cards with nonmatching numbers, indicating contrasting aliases.

Puentes' attire was not what one would wear to the Department of Homeland Security. Instead, he left the compound wearing a black hooded sweatshirt, black shorts, and black tennis shoes. He made sure to pack the car with an extra pair of black boots and socks, jeans and two white shirts, a towel, his flip cell phone, $54, and a plastic bag. He was ready to sit and wait.

The older model white Honda Civic registered to Puentes' uncle from Lyman, South Carolina made its way down the interstate through Spartanburg towards Atlanta. It was 4 a.m. He was on schedule.

CHAPTER 21
The Divorce

Alpharetta, Georgia
May 2011

I n Georgia, if one wants to end a marriage, he or she must file a complaint for divorce in the Superior Court. The individual can either hire an attorney who will prepare and file the case, or the individual can use the sample forms included in a packet and represent him or herself in court.

The following steps must be taken in Puentes in April and asked him to move out. He wanted to remain in Georgia, so he found temporary lodging in Lyman, South Carolina, until his immigration status was final.

The plaintiff's original petition was entered on May 9, 2011. The divorce proceedings for Vanda and Puentes were underway. He had no reason to stay married to her since his immigration status was about to change.

Vanda attended the meeting that day in May and stood before the judge in Superior Court of Fulton County. The case initiation form, notice of hearing, and the clerk's order of service by publication documents were filed. Her court date was assigned for the divorce hearing, May 23, 2011. She paid her $218.50 fee with the remaining balance of $219.00 to be paid once the case was settled. She had no reason to believe it would be dismissed. The divorce would be granted in her mind.

CHAPTER 22
Facing Evil

Duluth, Georgia
May 2011

The school year of 2010 - 2011 was coming to a close. We were all counting down the days, students and teachers alike. My family college planning meetings scheduled for 7 a.m. were winding down. The main focus for the last few days was final exams and graduation.

The radio alarm went off promptly at 5:30 a.m. as usual. This day I was sluggish. I stayed in bed, ignoring the nudges from the wet cat nose that nuzzled my hand. He wanted to be fed. I clicked the remote control until I found the news and weather on TV. I took a minute to review my work schedule for the day in my brain. Yes, today was different. No counseling meetings were on the docket, which meant I could stay in bed just a little longer. I couldn't wait for summer vacation so I could sleep in until sunrise.

Thirty minutes had gone by, and now I was indeed running late. What was I wearing? It was taking longer than usual to decide. It was 6:15 a.m., and I was out of time. I hurried down the hallway to the kitchen, throwing open the sliding glass door, encouraging the cat to take a quick loop. The sound of the can opener buzzed while I ran the water to make coffee.

I shouted, "Catnip, time to come back in. I'm running late. Let's go!" He did not respond to my command. After all, Catnip was the King-of-Cats. He moved at his own pace. I would have to get him inside later. I pulled the door closed without putting the pin in and made my way down the hallway back to the bedroom and to the shower.

I left the TV running so I could hear the weather, ran the water until it was hot, and jumped in for a quick shower. Suddenly the room went black. There was a slight bit of light from the light of dawn coming through the blinds. There were no sounds at all. The room was silent.

"What…a power shortage? I don't have time for this," I said aloud.

Quickly I turned off the shower and peered through the lace shower curtain. What was that? It looked like a shadow moving in front of the doorway. Was someone standing there? I pulled back the curtain to see a figure, a large, looming figure. A monster, I thought. My mind did not comprehend my circumstance. It didn't look human.

The knife-wielding intruder held the butcher knife over his head and covered his face with his black, padded glove. He wore a dark hooded sweatshirt to hide his appearance. The figure was menacing and evil. I screamed in sheer fright. What was happening? He aimed the butcher knife at my heart. It seemed unreal; all too surreal. Screaming again, I dropped to the bottom of the tub. I remember being told to fall to the ground as a form of self-defense when threatened. Of course, that was a plan for protecting yourself in a public place if you feared you were being kidnapped.

I pleaded for my life: "Please, please don't kill me."

How was I going to defend myself here, cornered in a tub? There was nowhere to go. I pulled down the shower curtain from the wall and tried to use the rod to keep distance between the two of us. That would last for a second. He pulled the rod from my grip. The plastic curtain draped over my dripping wet body that was reeling in pain from the fall. Again, I pleaded for my life. I thought I was about to die in the tub only to be found dripping in my own blood.

Staring down the tip of the blade I thought, I can't die today. I have too much to live for. I am not going out this way, I thought. I prayed; pleaded with God to take care of me. Help me, God help me. I pleaded for life again.

He stepped in the tub and stood over me. My focus was on the point of the knife. Was I out of time?

To my surprise, the attacker grabbed my wet hair and told me to "shut up." He had an accent.

The attacker pulled me to the bedroom with his gloved hand over my mouth, holding the butcher knife blade to my neck.

I tried to speak, but he quickly said, "Do not talk."

Yes, he had an accent, a Spanish accent. He stood taller than my 5'7" stature. His face and eyes were dark. That was all I could see. I tried to make mental notes.

I had to think quickly; I knew what was coming. How would I survive the upcoming event, which was most likely going to be a rape and/or a stabbing? There was no time to waste. This would be my only chance to save myself. I had to get to my nightstand.

The sexual predator threw me to the bed. My mind was racing as he directed me to move back. This won't happen to me I thought. I am not going down like this. I am not going to be raped, stabbed, and left for dead.

"I have money, lots of money, right here in my nightstand," I said. I inched back slowly towards the headboard, making my way closer to the only chance I would have to defend myself, closer to my firearm.

Again, I nervously stated, "I have money, lots of money, over here." I thought he would stand still at the foot of my bed while I moved toward the drawer; I was mistaken. He drew closer. I inched up towards the pillows and swung my legs over the side of the bed. His knees now touched mine as he held the knife over my head. I slowly pulled the drawer open.

Luckily, the attacker had turned off the lights, and it was still dark in the room at 6:30 a.m. No one would have been able to make out what was in that drawer, I thought. He did not speak a word, but he slowly placed his gloved hand inside the dresser and moved it over the items within. He pulled his hand out; I was frozen in fear. I could not breathe. I did not want to let him know how I felt. I needed to remain calm. Would he pull out one of my three pistols? He did not.

"I'll get it now," I said, referring to the money. He remained silent and nodded. He allowed me to proceed. Thank goodness he was greedy.

Slowly I placed my hand into the drawer and felt for a gun. My hand slid around a grip. It was my .22 caliber, the target pistol, the one with the gold trigger, engraved wooden handle, and 5 1/2 inch barrel. It had the longest barrel of the three weapons with the smallest bullets of the bunch. I would have to use this one, but how would I get this one out of the drawer without making a sound?

Somehow, I was given the strength to continue. I moved gingerly and bent my wrist to maneuver the barrel. I prayed the safety was off. My attacker continued to hold the butcher knife over my head. Since the drawer was only open three inches, I would have to maneuver the handle and barrel slowly and precisely as to not knock the side or top of the stand. I could not make a sound or I risked being murdered on the spot.

Suddenly, the pistol was out. I turned my wrist at a 90-degree angle and raised the weapon with one continuous motion towards the predator. The flash lit up the room as I pulled the trigger. Thank goodness Jim had made all of the handguns "hot" the last time he was over. Was that choice a premonition or a spiritual intervention? I did not know.

I could not see him. I did not have my glasses on. Where was he? I fired again, and again. I saw the flash, but I did not hear a sound. Seven flashes, and he still stood there with the knife raised above his head in my direction; he had moved back several steps. He never said a word. He held one of his gloved hands to his chest. Was he indicating he was wearing a bulletproof vest? Again, he made no sound. I did not know if he would lunge toward me or not. Did I even hit him? I would be out of bullets in a few seconds and he would kill me for sure.

It was then I focused on his hooded head and pulled the trigger. He flinched; I missed. He had dodged the bullet and moved in front of the doorway. A tiny hole was left in the wall where I had aimed for his head. I had two bullets left. He made a sudden movement, and I fired my last two rounds. He still had the knife in his hands, but this time he turned to run down the hallway.

Would he return? The gun was empty and he knew it. I screamed in terror, "Damn!"

Quickly I turned to my nightstand before he would return. I had the emptied Buckmark in one hand and a loaded .38 revolver in the other. My goal was to get to safety; to get out of my house to a neighbor's house. In a state of panic, I mistakenly dropped the loaded .38 in the hallway and was left with the empty one when I rounded the corner. As I made this realization that I was holding an empty pistol, I dropped that one, too, in the kitchen. I caught a glimpse of him outside of the back door and pulled it closed and pinned it. I did not want him to come back in. I needed time to escape.

Grabbing the cordless phone from the living room, I scrambled out the front door to vacate the premises. It would take him a minute to catch up with me if he ran from the backside of the house to the front.

Looking left and right, I noticed my neighbor's garage door was open. I breezed by him as he smoked a cigarette and collapsed on their kitchen floor.

"Help me. Someone tried to kill me. I don't know where he is. Please help me!" I screamed in pain and fear.

My neighbor and his wife came to my aid and called 911 to report the attack. I got on the line to share my experience, the attempt on my life, and my injuries. The attacker, the rapist, the knife-wielding intruder, had fled out the back door, I reported. I did not know where he was.

The Aftermath

CHAPTER 23
The Swarm

Duluth, Georgia
May 2011

The Gwinnett County Police Department sent out the dispatch alert and the announcement hit the airways. The CAD (Computer Aided Dispatch) call went out at 6:30 a.m. The neighborhood was swarming with police cars from both the night and day shifts.

"Possible burglary in progress," the 911 operator reported. "Hear women in the background crying hysterically. She is speaking with neighbor." The dispatcher was multitasking, listening to my responses while communicating with the police responding to the scene.

The notification continued. "An intruder had entered the house without permission and left the house after his attack."

"Copy that. Arriving on scene," the officer reported.

"House to the right of where the call was coming from," the dispatcher stated.

"Female was in shower and lights turned off. Male had an accent. She shot him and he ran out back door… attacker male, had on hoodie, dark skinned with an accent," the operator reported.

"Copy," the officer said.

"Notify K-9 Unit to check area for other perpetrators. Clearing house," another officer stated.

"The victim does not know where he went. There are still handguns in the house and shots have been fired," 911 Operator noted.

The first few officers arrived on the scene. Several made their way into the house while others went around the back. The front door was open, so the police quickly entered.

The interior of the house had been cleared and crackle of the radio indicated another officer had spotted the suspect in the back deck area. The officer inside could see the point of entry, the back door. As he approached the door and looked to the right where he, too, saw the suspect.

"Have visual on perpetrator," officer stated. He tried to open the door but the latch was not working. The officer did not see the pin at the base of the door and used his baton to smash the glass.

"Need CSI, ambulance, Fire Department," a second officer requested.

The sirens from the ambulances and fire engines woke up the rest of the inhabitants of the subdivision.

The attacker wore a black hooded sweatshirt, black shorts, black athletic shoes, and thick, black padded gloves. A butcher knife was found several feet from him. He apparently had been shot, the officer reported. Several officers began performing CPR, while another called for an ambulance. The suspect was immediately placed on a gurney and wheeled to an emergency vehicle for transport.

"Need CID (Crime Investigation Department), contact Homicide," officer reported.

By this time, multiple layers of yellow crime scene tape secured the area. There were some quick questions from the police on the scene. The conscientious and professional men and women in blue would shield me from the news media who wanted to expose my identity and my life-threatening experience on the spot.

The news station reporters closed in around the area with their vans, antenna, cameras, zoom lenses, microphones, and notepads, all trying to be the first to get the story.

Emergency Medical Service technicians assisted me into the back of the ambulance while I was shielded from site by several police officers. Immediately my vitals were taken and a quick assessment was made. The back pain and neck strain were excruciating. Sinus Tachycardia was noted on the report probably due to the pain and fear. The EMT pumped up the cuff and noted my blood pressure was racing. An IV was inserted into my arm in case medication for pain needed to be administered on the way to the hospital. I was afraid I would be brought to the same medical facility as my attacker. I was afraid that he could still try to kill me. The sirens sounded and the ambulances left the scene, one for a hospital down the road, the other headed to a facility cross-town.

By 7:30 a.m., the story had hit the airwaves. News talk radio was already reporting. "An unidentified woman was attacked by a knife-wielding intruder in her home while in the shower early this morning."

The police would continue to canvas the neighborhood. From the assailant's pockets, they had recovered a cell phone and keys to a Honda.

"Suspicious vehicle found on corner of Landington and Sinecure Way."

The police located the car parked a street away from my residence. They uncovered Puentes' paperwork issued by the Department of Homeland Security noting his address on N.

Bridges Rd, Alpharetta, Georgia. Along with these documents, the police uncovered multiple forms of identification under various aliases, two different social security cards and two alien registration numbers. They also found a change of clothing, including an extra pair of black boots and socks, jeans and two white shirts, a flip cell phone, and a plastic bag. The car was impounded and towed by Statewide Wrecker Service.

The two detectives quickly scoured the home while Crime Scene Investigation (CSI) units moved in. One detective would stay on the premises while the other reported to the hospital. CSI would soon begin their work inside the crime scene, my home. Their job was to put the pieces of the puzzle together while not destroying any evidence. It was all beginning to make sense that a sexual predator had committed an attack on an innocent victim.

CHAPTER 24
Hospital Tour

Duluth, Georgia
May 2011

At 7:45 a.m. the nurse entered the room for the first time. Vitals were taken, followed by the initial assessment of my complaints and report of pains. The doctor finally entered, wrote up his notes, and requested further examination for back and neck injuries, and foot pain. A C-spine and LS-spine x-rays were ordered to check my back, neck, and ribcage. The cut on my foot was tended to as well. It took about 30 minutes to complete the scans. My vitals continued to be monitored every 15 minutes.

Medication was prescribed, but I requested to hold off until my statement could be taken. I wanted to be sure I was clear with the facts when I spoke to the police.

I was left alone for what seemed a lifetime. What was happening? What would happen to me? How could I get in touch with my family?

Two police officers had escorted me to the hospital. They were assigned to stay close by. A policewoman came in first and asked for phone numbers of people I wanted to contact. They could not find my cell phone in the house. I located my numbers printed on a paper in my wallet. Good thing I thought to do this. I could not think of anyone's number. She tried to calm my nerves.

"He will come and get me," I said in fear. She could not say anything, but I could tell by the look on her face that something had happened.

"You are safe now," she calmly replied.

"How can you be sure?" I asked.

She just smiled and said, "You will be okay. You did what you had to do to save your life."

The next visitor was her partner who was on his first week of duty. He quietly sat in a chair at the foot of the bed. I was still in a state of shock, and it seemed like hours had passed. The patrolman seemed uncomfortable, so I tried to make conversation to put him at ease; that was the counselor in me.

I asked, "Have you ever used your gun while on duty?" He shook his head no.

I remained frightened, and he sat patiently waiting for the next order. Soon he was called from the room.

I was left alone again waiting for the next visitor. Meanwhile, I was creating a list of questions to which I needed answers. Thoughts were racing through my brain. Too many things didn't add up. With nothing but time on my hands, I wondered: How did I survive? How and when could I make contact with my fiancé, my family, and my friends, including my priest? What was going to happen next? I had just defended my life. Would I need a lawyer?

CHAPTER 25
The Interrogations

Duluth, Georgia
May 2011

Corporal D. Hennelly, a detective from the Gwinnett County Police Criminal Investigations Homicide and Assault Unit, arrived at my home by mid-morning. Multiple police cars were still parked on the street. He signed himself in through the access log at the crime scene and took out his pen and booklet. He would be taking notes on what he observed. The landscape was well maintained around the entry points. He walked through the front door and was greeted by CSI who was already processing the scene.

The detective proceeded around to the back of the home where he noted the landscaping which was maintained as well as the front yard. He eyed the porch and deck, the scene where the suspect was apprehended. It was easy to approach the backyard from the streets, he thought. It was in the backyard that he found a towel neatly folded. This did not match the rest of the surroundings.

Next, the detective entered the home through what was left of the shattered sliding glass door and sketched the house plan, recording where various experiences took place and where evidence was found. He examined the pulled down shower curtain and scrutinized the black streaks in the tub. He surmised that the marks were made from black soled athletic shoes the assailant was wearing. The television was on *ABC News* with the sound turned to the off position, and bullet casings were located around the nightstand. The bed was made.

Crouching down to look under the bed for clues, the detective found Catnip hunkering down in fear. He reached in to grab the animal thinking he would bring it to the neighbor's house for safekeeping, but Catnip sank the only four teeth the twenty-year-old cat had left into the hand of the detective. The cat was not about to be moved. He left it alone, brought it some food and the cat box and asked the CSI agents to close the door to keep the cat in the room. He had no doubt the notes from investigators would be thorough and complete including measurements, fingerprints, number of casings, and a list of items related to the crime.

Detective Hennelly and his comrade made their way to the hospital for my initial interview. One sat at the foot of the bed and the other closer to me.

"We are here for a statement, to try and figure out how the attack occurred, the timing, and the threat level. I'm Detective Hennelly and this is Sergeant Shaw," he said.

I nodded an acknowledgement of their task and greeting.

"I purposely avoided the pain medication so I could be clear with my statements," I shared.

"Yes, the doctor informed us of this. Good. Let's get started. I will be recording this so I am sure to have your comments noted correctly. Is that okay with you?" he asked.

I nodded and responded. "I need your help, and I want you to catch this man."

"First of all, I want you to know your cat is safe in your bedroom. I found him during the search process and he sank his teeth into me when I tried to reach for him," he shared.

"He is up to date with his shots," I assured him.

"I will be taking notes as well," he stated.

Shaking, I recalled my experience being as detailed as possible with my explanation from start to finish, from the time the lights went out to my escape to safety. Several points surprised even me.

I explained what I saw when I opened the shower curtain, a man with a knife dressed in a hoodie with dark clothes and gloves.

The detective said, "Yes, we have the butcher knife he held over you. It came from your collection in the kitchen."

"What? My knife? He used my knife?" I was surprised and confused.

"Yes, he dropped it as he was running through the kitchen and out the back door," he said.

I explained, "I was running late for the first time in months. I let the cat out and did not put the pin back in the door thinking I would grab the cat later. Next thing I knew, the lights went out. There were no sounds. I imagined there was a power outage."

I continued my description of the events one after another including how I pleaded for my life and offered money as a distraction. "I was amazed the attacker did not feel any of the guns in the nightstand drawer when I remembered that the attacker was wearing thickly padded gloves. That made perfect sense. The fact that the intruder had turned off the lights was another blessing in disguise as he could not see what was inside the nightstand."

The report continued. "I ran out of bullets and the rapist knew it. He heard me react to the blank click of the empty pistol." I explained that I reached for another weapon for fear that the rapist would return as quickly as he had exited. In a state of panic, I dropped the loaded one and arrived in the kitchen with an empty weapon.

"I saw him briefly out the back door, pulled it closed, grabbed a phone, and ran to the safety of my neighbor's house. I did not know where he went after that," I said.

The interview was complete.

"We will take the Buckmark as evidence, but we have no reason to take your other two registered pistols," the detective commented.

That was a relief. I feared there could be retaliation if this incident had been gang related.

There was one more piece of news for clarification – the police had located the assailant on the back porch with the butcher knife close by. The detective made his last announcement. "The sexual predator, your attacker, has expired. We will be looking into his history to see if he had attacked other victims. You probably were not the first."

The threat was over; however, the memories of terror would live on. According to the detectives, there would be no charges pending at this time. The two men left the room.

It was at that moment that I prayed for all the women this man had probably raped, assaulted, and terrorized in the past, possibly even murdered. I hoped these victims would receive the news from their police department that this man would no longer come to their doors to terrorize them over and over again. I prayed for myself and amazingly enough, I prayed to God to deal with this devil of a human being as He would each of us in the end. The counselor in me recognized my attacker was probably a sociopath with antisocial behaviors, possibly a serial rapist or murderer, and definitely a sexual predator. Thoughts raced through my head.

The nurse walked in one last time and I accepted the offer for medication to handle my pain. It was a level ten on a scale from one to ten, ten being the worst pain.

CHAPTER 26
Interviews and Search Warrants

Duluth, Georgia
May 2011

Several search warrants were secured from the Gwinnett County Magistrate Court for the rapist's car, his personal items, and his residence. The vehicle, a four-door 1998 Honda Civic, white in color with South Carolina tags, was registered to Puentes' uncle, Ricardo Ruiz, of Lyman, South Carolina.

Detective Hennelly made contact with Puentes' relatives in Lyman. Maria Jarez, the cousin who allowed Puentes to use the car, said that he had told her he had an appointment in

Atlanta with the Immigration Office of Homeland Security to have his fingerprints taken. She had no reason to doubt him, as she had known him for ten or more years while she lived in Cuba. She and his uncle said that Puentes had been living in the U.S. for three or four years. Maria gave the detective Puentes' wife's name and phone number and noted she would contact his family about his demise. She would retrieve the car from the impound lot in the next two weeks.

The detective and his crew removed a box of items that belonged to Puentes from the car, hoping to find clues to other open investigations.

Next was contact with my fiancé, Jim. The detective needed to cover all of the bases; he kept scrupulous notes. He dialed his number and the questioning began.

"Good morning, sir. My name is Detective Hennelly with the Gwinnett County Police and I am investigating the attack on your fiancé this morning. Do you have a moment to answer some questions?"

Among Detective Hennelly's questions were, "How did the victim learn how to shoot?"

"I taught her to shoot three years ago in South Carolina. I'm a retired Lieutenant Colonel from the United States Air Force and still work on base. We shoot over here at our range. We met while earning our doctorates at the University."

The detective was satisfied with his inquiry at that time. Jim offered he would be in Duluth the following week. There was no need for further questions as the detective would see him then.

Alpharetta, Georgia, was the next stop Detective Hennelly would make – a visit to speak with Puentes' estranged wife, Vanda. She was not helpful according to the detective except to say that they had married on July 10, 2010, filed for separation in April of 2011, filed the petition for divorce on May 9, and expected to go to court May 23 to finalize the process. Vanda, however, did speak to the news media on camera, stating her estranged husband had committed a crime in Johns

Creek, another Atlanta suburb, a few months earlier.

Detective Hennelly headed back to Duluth to interview the victim's neighbors. The Wisecoff's, the people who helped me that morning, were first on the list. They described what they experienced as I ran into their house and what I had shared about the incident. Rebecca also shared she had spotted what she thought was a white Camry three different times on the road in front of our homes while out for a smoke in the previous weeks. The last time she observed the car, she thought it was suspicious as the car made a quick three-point turn when it had been noticed.

The Tolland's on the other side of my home kept to themselves. They had not heard a sound or seen anything suspicious.

Johnny, from across the street, commented on seeing a figure in the dark on foot in front of our homes on two different occasions over the past two weeks. His dog had chased him down the road both times.

Neil, my neighbor who lived down the street, commented on seeing the white car with

South Carolina plates parked in front of a vacant lot about 1:30 a.m. the previous weekend. He just figured a neighbor he did not know must have friends in from out of town frequently.

Detective Hennelly continued his research. An effort was made nationwide to link Puentes to any other open cases via a BOLO (Be on the Look Out or All-Points Bulletin). He was able to track him from his point of entry in Laredo, Texas on December 26, 2008, to Florida, to Nebraska, and then Georgia. Nine criminal records were found in the database as recently as two months prior to this incident. He would follow up using CODIS, the Combined DNA Index System, to see if the perpetrator was involved in any other unsolved investigations.

CHAPTER 27
Visitors Allowed

Duluth, Georgia
May 2011

The waiting was difficult. Finally, the nurse let me know I had several visitors. One was a priest, a good soul, and the other, a close friend.

Fr. John Wadkins was greeted by Detective Hennelly in the hospital lobby. They exchanged brief introductions.

"This was a bad man, and I am fearful he has offended many times," the detective said.

My priest appeared in the doorway. "Thank you so much for coming," I said.

We hugged, and I cried. I told Fr. John how the events unfolded. He listened.

"Too many things don't add up. How did I survive the attack, the attempted rape and attempt on my life?" I questioned.

"The only thought that made sense to me at that moment was one of spiritual intervention," I explained. "I felt like I was in a bubble, protected; every action seemed as if it was in slow motion and deliberate. I felt guided by a power greater than myself."

Fr. John focused on me as I told my story.

"I was very lucky that the intruder turned the lights out, that he was greedy and wanted money before he proceeded with his intended torture, and that he wore gloves... he did not feel the handguns in the nightstand."

"I remained calm even with the knife towering over me. How could that be? Somehow, I kept my wits and survived." The priest continued to listen to my thoughts.

"How many people had battled with this predator over the years?" I explained to the priest. "I saw no face, just evil in the attacker's eyes. He wasn't human."

"So many questions have been streaming through my mind. Was my survival due to quick thinking, luck, or faith? I think it may have been a little of each. I don't know, but I thanked God for letting me live. I prayed for this man's soul, if he had one," I rambled on.

Fr. John explained to me how he felt when he heard the news. "We had just finished Mass and I was approached by the assistant principal who had taken the phone call from the police woman who contacted the school. She explained what had occurred and I had to sit down on the steps. I was trying to comprehend what you had experienced. I wasn't sure how I could help you or what I was going to say. Then driving to the hospital it came to me that I just needed to listen, to pray, and to be with you. I remembered this feeling and what I did for others who had been involved in a traumatic case such as yours when I was a police chaplain back in New Zealand."

"Thank goodness you were able to get here. I can't thank you enough." I smiled though still shaking from the experience.

"I marvel at your strength and courage," he stated.

The good Father made no judgments, consoled me, and listened to my thoughts. He offered to escort me back to my home when the doctor wrote the release and he left the room to get his car.

The door to my emergency room opened slowly. It was my next visitor. I was greeted by two sets of welcoming arms, my good friend Teresa Williams and her mother.

Hugs and tears were exchanged. Still shaking I sobbed, "It was him or me. I did what I had to do to survive." They held me tight. I summarized the events of the morning and they listened attentively.

Teresa recalled how she was contacted. "First a policewoman said, 'She has been in an accident and has asked for you to come to the hospital.' Then she said, 'There had been an event at her home and she was injured.' She could not be specific with details because they had not been specific with you yet. I couldn't believe what was happening. When I got to the lobby, I met the policewoman who made the initial call. She said something to the effect of, 'Please let her know we have been trying to stop this man. She did what we could not do. You should be proud of the way she protected her life in self-defense.'"

These two incredible women, Teresa and her mom, would be my angels in the next part of my journey along with Fr. John. I couldn't have been in better hands.

Plans were made for me to leave the hospital and to return to my home, the scene of the crime. The nurse returned with a wheelchair and I was about to embark in good company of Teresa, her mom, and my police chaplain friend, Fr. John.

CHAPTER 28
The Crime Scene Investigation

Duluth, Georgia
May 2011

The pain was still outrageous even with medication in my system. Fr. John pulled up next to Teresa's car in his PT Cruiser. Exiting the parking lot, we headed to my home a few miles down the road. What we did not expect on my street was the parade of television and radio station vans and police cars that continued to hug the curbs.

Each reporter was stationed with long-range lens to catch a view of anyone entering or leaving my home. They were instructed and constantly reminded by the police to stay behind the yellow crime scene tape.

Our caravan stopped at the edge of the driveway and the police told us to head up the road and wait until they were ready for my arrival. "You will want to cover your license plate so the reporters cannot access your tag information," the officer suggested.

Our two cars parked next to each other waiting for the signal. Teresa quickly pulled a sock over her plates. A call to her cell phone rang through.

"You can come back now," the lead officer said. "Be sure to cover your face so the media cannot take your picture. This is a sexual assault case and we will maintain your privacy and not release your name."

Like ants that smell sweets, the camera operators and photographers began to creep closer to the protected property. Fr. John stepped out of his vehicle and distracted the media, while the three of us prepared to emerge from the Mustang.

Six men and women in uniform created a human barricade between the news media and me. It was then that I opened the door, covered my face, and was escorted inside my home. The clicking of the cameras could be heard in the distance.

The crime scene investigators were still boxing up their materials as we entered. Decked out in their yellow and black CSI jackets, they buzzed through my home. Yellow cones with numbers were set next to each piece of evidence, including the butcher knife, the bullet casings, firearms, the shower rod, fingerprints, and black rubber shoe marks in the tub. They had searched through every square inch of my home and sifted through my belongings. Fingerprint residue highlighted my walls, doorways, light switches, and bath. They had removed the shower curtain and rod, and towels for evidence. In the bedroom, they had measured the distance between the tub to the bed, furniture and the bullet casings, and so forth.

Each officer offered words of comfort. "You are a brave lady." "You did the right thing by protecting your life." "Thank you for protecting others from becoming his next victim."

Still in shock, I wandered about my home. Would things ever calm down? Why was my sliding glass door shattered? It was so confusing. I could only think small. I just wanted to be comfortable in my own skin, my own clothes, and find my fur-ball, Catnip.

As the police wrapped up their work, the lead officer let me know what would happen next. "We will send a biohazard worker to your home to be sure everything is taken care of. You don't have to do a thing. The door window was broken when one of the officers used his baton. The glass company is on their way to replace it and fix the latch lock. Lastly, when we leave, we will have to take down the yellow crime scene tape. This means the reporters may approach your front door. All you have to do is tell them to leave your property. If they do not, call us and we will be sure they do or they will be arrested."

I thanked her for her explanation and waited for the next visitors to arrive.

Neighbors stopped by to offer their support, the phone rang off the hook, and emails flooded my inbox. My approach to recovery would be one day at a time.

CHAPTER 29
The News Media Descend

Duluth, Georgia
May – June 2011

One after another, the reporters approached my home with not a minute to spare. They stepped up to my door, rang the bell, and hoped for a scoop for the 7 a.m., noon, 5 p.m., and 11 p.m. news hour reports. Each time they were turned away by my family and friends.

My trauma intensified due to the constant contact by the news media. Photos of the intruder hit the screen by noon the day of the attack. Puentes was identified as a 34-year-old Cuban national. Follow-up stories focused on his crimes in years past, including a reported eight felony convictions. I remained frightened and worried about this individual's contacts and how they may react.

Headlines read, "Showering Woman Shoots Intruder, Victim Flees to Neighbor," "Home Invader Killed," "Kidnapping, Murder and Mayhem: Intended Rape Victim Kills Attacker," and "Woman Fatally Shoots Intruder." Each station had a group of young men and women who camped outside my home for what seemed like weeks, though it was only days. I would not turn on the television or listen to the radio for several weeks.

At first, each station would send their headline news reporter who placed his and herself at the edge of the driveway hoping to capture an image of me, the victim, along with a comment from the most horrific story of the day. They would hold up pictures of Puentes as they spoke to the camera lens.

Channel 2 News was one of the first to report starting with their headline:

Police: Woman Shot Intruder 9 Times In Self Defense; School Counselor Shoots, Kills Home Intruder

An intruder who was shot and killed after a confrontation with a Duluth woman in her shower was likely stalking her for days and may have other victims, Gwinnett police said.

The 53-year-old woman, who is also a veteran private school counselor, was alone at the time of the Wednesday morning attack. She lives on Mount Tabor Circle in Duluth.

The woman was getting out of the shower when she was met by a strange man with a kitchen knife, police said. They said there was a struggle in the bathroom, and she fell in the tub. Police later identified the man as Israel Perez Puentes, a Cuban national who lived in Alpharetta.

"The male was armed with a kitchen knife; a struggle ensued between the two of them. She fell in the bathtub injuring herself," Gwinnett police spokesman Edwin Ritter said.

The woman tried to fight the man off with a shower rod, and he forced her into her bedroom, police said. They said she told her attacker she had money in the room. But, she grabbed a .22-caliber handgun and shot the man nine times, police said.

Police said the man ran out of a back door and collapsed in the yard. He later died at the Gwinnett Medical Center. The victim, who was injured in the scuffle, was also taken to the hospital for treatment of non-life-threatening injuries. Police have not released her name.

Police told Channel 2's Kerry Kavanaugh they don't know why the woman was targeted.

"He may have seen her somewhere and he identified her as being a potential victim and he basically stalked her until he found the right moment to act on it," said Ritter.

"Our department is looking into any other cases around the metro Atlanta area as well as our jurisdiction to see if he may be involved with any other sexual assaults that may have occurred."

Ritter said the shooting investigation was ongoing but defended the victim, saying the shooting appeared to be justified, and that she acted in self-defense. He said there are no plans to charge her.

Police said Thursday that neighbors had spotted Puentes' car in the neighborhood several days before the attack but did not report it. Puentes' estranged wife told Kavanaugh he had been arrested for burglary in Johns Creek in December.

Spontaneous interviews were conducted with passersby.

Neighbor Rebecca Wisecoff said, she woke up to screams and crying. At first, she thought it was her young son, until she walked down the hallway. "I found our neighbor lying naked on our kitchen floor, wet and screaming that someone tried to kill her and that she had shot him," Wisecoff said through swelling tears. "She didn't know if he had run away or what happened, but she managed to get out of the house and into our house," Wisecoff added. "She was just inconsolable and a pile on our kitchen floor."

Dan Turer, a friend and neighbor, said he was amazed at how the victim defended herself against the armed intruder. "She's smart, she's witty, and obviously well prepared," he said.

Another neighbor Mike Grove drove by to offer his support. "Excellent! Yes, anybody by herself like that that can put him down with a .22...she must be a good shot."

"I would love to meet her!" said Jessica Oliver, who lives nearby. "It's amazing that she could react like that and not freak out."

"That's awesome that she had something to protect herself with," neighbor Michelle Churn said. "I don't know how she was good enough to get her gun like that. She's very lucky and fortunate that she was able to defend herself. Good for her."

Marsha Daily, who lives down the street, said her house has been broken into twice since she moved into the neighborhood 11 years ago. "Fortunately, I wasn't home either time, but I've lost a lot of stuff because of break-ins," Daily said.

As time passed, the stations continued to send reporters seemingly without any regard for my feelings.

Onlookers continued to travel past my house each day. Some ogled as they walked their dogs, while others drove by slowly just peering out their car windows and pointing.

A week passed when I received a call from the public relations officer at the police department. Corporal Ritter said, "The good news is that your case has been closed as one of self-defense. I am sorry to tell you that we must release the 911 tape since it is public record now. Only one news station has been asking for the tape each day, *Channel 2*. All others chose to not share this recording; they did not want to cause you any other emotional stress. I am sorry you will have to go through this exposure."

The story had been on the news constantly, it seemed, and in the local newspaper *The Atlanta Constitution,* for a week or two. Reporters chose only the words they wanted to focus on: "I shot him as much as I could" said one headline, taking my statement out of context from the 911 call. I had to ignore this. It was a secondary trauma to my horrific event. How cruel it seemed.

I received a phone call from a friend. "I'm in a gun store here in Connecticut, and while I was standing at the register I looked up and there was your story, a newspaper article from the *Atlanta Constitution*, on the wall. It did not mention your name."

"Are you serious…up north, too?" I said.

"Yes, and I was proud to say I know you! The owners wish you well and are so glad you are safe," he said.

Commenters debated online and expressed views such as "Women with Guns; Rapist Beware," "Woman with Gun 1 – Rapist with Knife 0," and "Georgia Teacher Safe, Would-Be Rapist Dead…Thanks to a Gun."

I made a conscious decision to avoid some TV news stations and newspapers from that day forward. I kept my blinds closed and had family and friends shoo away the reporters who knocked on my door. There was no need to hear my pain, my trauma, and my fear reported first hand again. I had struggled to live. I defended myself, and I survived. Going through it once was enough for me.

CHAPTER 30
Healing

Duluth, Georgia
May - June 2011

The cleansing of the house continued. Though I was in pain, I needed to prepare for the arrival of my family and friends. I needed to make it a safe place for all. They would be there to help me and I wanted to make sure they were comfortable. That was the counselor in me. One visitor after another brought a smile and a much welcomed and heartfelt hug, food, and even a blessing of my home.

At first, I did not want to leave the protection of my four walls for fear of more harassment by reporters. As each news van retreated to Atlanta and the passersby became bored with the events of the previous week, it became easier to venture outside. I would immediately install an alarm system. The people at A. R. Home Security Systems of Duluth were amazing. They were at my home the day I called with the complete system installed in a few hours.

I felt more secure about leaving my home with family members to seek treatment for physical pains, including medical updates, MRIs, CAT scans, physical therapy, and follow-up doctor visits. These appointments were the priority for the month. I recovered quickly at least physically, but the emotional scars would take a longer time to heal.

How would I go about healing my mind? I knew I needed to thank those who had helped me survive.

First, I stopped by the indoor gun range where I received instruction from a county policewoman and Tom, the instructor, in how to use a handgun for self-defense. I was greeted with a smile and a hug. "Come back and see us anytime," he said.

The second stop was to the Bass Pro Shop to thank John for selling me the target pistol that saved my life. John had a look of shock on his face as I recounted the events. He was relieved I was safe and offered his support, too.

The third and fourth stops were to the firehouse and police department to thank the many professionals that assisted me in my time of distress.

Lastly, I wanted to thank the professionals who were the first responders to the scene. I would send this letter to the powers in charge:

June 6, 2011

Criminal Investigations Division and Crime Scene: 770 Hi-Hope Road Lawrenceville, GA 30046

Central Police Precinct: 3125 Satellite Blvd, Duluth, Georgia 30096

Fire Station/Medic No. 19: 3275 N. Berkeley Lake Rd, Duluth, GA 30096

Dear Asst. Chief Michael Reonas, Major Kevin Moran, Sergeant Mr. John Suroweic #1291,

Lieutenant Jack Conley, Major Christa Spradley, and Fire Chief Bill Myers:

It is a pleasure to be able to write this letter of commendation for the many police, fire, and EMT personnel who helped me through an extremely difficult experience on the morning of May 11, 2011. As the news put it, a knife-wielding intruder entered my bathroom with the intentions of sexually assaulting me. I was blessed with a sound mind (though terrified), guidance from a power greater than myself, and training in the use of firearms in order to protect myself. I believe these three points allowed me to survive.

Thank you to the EMTs who assisted me in transport to the hospital. Each were kind and knowledgeable about treating a patient in a traumatic situation.

Though traumatized, I felt safe when surrounded by the extremely professional men and women of the Police and Fire Departments. I am proud to be a citizen of Gwinnett County and to be protected by these fine employees of the state.

Thank you to all of the policemen and woman involved in the case including the two uniformed officers who escorted and watched over me while in the Emergency Room, Leslie

Gibson #658 and Trenton Greene #1471, were instrumental in keeping me calm and feeling protected. Sergeant Steve Shaw#609 and Corporal Dennis Hennelly #1070 from the Criminal Investigations Division - Homicide/Assault Unit, were the two detectives assigned to take my statement and question me regarding the incident. They made sure I maintained my integrity while completing their work. Upon arriving home to a sea of news reporters, their vans set up as far as the eye could see, I was safe in the hands of Officer Sheila Moore #1291. She assisted me in gaining access to my home along with many other officers who guarded my privacy while shielding me from the camera's eye. Once I entered my home, personnel with the Crime Investigation Unit, Derek Foote, Beth Smith, and Krystal Kriegshauser under the direction of Jeff Branyon, welcomed me with compassion and maintained a professional demeanor while collecting evidence at the scene. There were numerous other officers throughout the various shifts including Z. Falkenberry #1412, J.T. Smith #1054, J. Yarbrough #1352, J. Santiago #1122, Sergeant Rich Long #439, M.J. Etheridge #1359, M.G. Ward #1322, Officer Robinson PS, and many more who made sure my property and home were secured. Victims

Assistance was contacted by the police and came to my aid in replacing my door and cleaning up the scene.

Detective Corporal Hennelly was instrumental in helping me to better understand the events and the process, while Corporal Ed Ritter assisted me with media issues such as the notification of the release of the 911 tape. That gave me time to prepare for another onslaught of media attention.

I apologize if I missed recognizing anyone who may have helped me that day. I hope you will share this letter with all that were involved.

Thank you all once again for your understanding and professional approach in handling this horrific event - Gwinnett is surely great!

My Best Regards

The police continued to watch my home for the next month. The rookie who sat in the emergency room with me was assigned to peruse my neighborhood. "If you ever write a book about this experience, please let me know. I want all the women in my life to know how you handled yourself so they can take care of themselves in the future."

"I sure will," I said, knowing it would be a while before that would happen.

CHAPTER 31
The Plot Unfolds

Duluth, Georgia
June 2011

It was Wednesday, two weeks after the flurry of activity, when Detective Hennelly arrived at my home.

"How are you feeling today?" he asked.

"It's one day at a time," I explained.

"Do you feel like taking a walk around your home," he asked.

"Sure," I responded. Still sore from my fall, we slowly made our way out the back door. I hoped to get some answers.

We toured the outside of my home while he discussed what he had found.

"You have a lovely yard. I noticed it was well manicured front and back." Then he asked, "Would you have left a towel neatly folded in the backyard?"

"No," I responded as chills ran up and down my spine.

"Look at this location," he said, as he pointed to the spot where the towel was found. "The material was placed directly behind those bushes which blocked Puentes from site of the neighbor's kitchen windows. I expect he sat here to watch your movements. After speaking with your neighbors who have two dogs, I believe the attacker watched your window for your lights to turn on. He probably took note for several days or even weeks. He chose this time of day because the dogs were not released until seven o'clock each morning."

Next, the detective pointed to the bathroom window. "Puentes could watch your lights come on and off in your rooms. He knew your schedule to the exact moment you let your cat out every morning onto the back porch."

I felt sick. How did I not know I was being watched? I wondered if he had ever murdered any of his victims.

The next bit of information was interesting, too. Detective Hennelly went on to report, "We found car keys in his pocket to the white Honda which was parked in the street behind your house. Puentes walked through the bushes to his spot probably more than once."

"Had my neighbors even noticed this strange car parked there more than a day with out-of-state plates?" I asked.

"Indeed they had, but they did not think to question it. They thought someone was visiting from out of town," he explained.

As we walked back to the house, the detective pointed to the latch on my screened in porch. He placed his hand through a small hole made in the screen. "Your attacker pulled the screen from the edge which allowed him to unhook the latch. Puentes must have scoped out your premises over a period of at least a month," he said.

We sat down in the living room. The detective shared his research concerning the Puentes' history. The story began to unfold and the list was long. The charges ranged from terroristic threats, sexual assault, armed robbery, and to attempted murder in the state of Nebraska. The intruder spent only 67 days in jail since the victims feared for their lives and did not testify. I understood their fear all too well.

"We also have him connected to attacks in Florida, South Carolina, and Georgia," Detective Hennelly revealed.

Then the detective went on. "We found a couple of applications for citizenships in his car, several driver licenses from states using at least four unique aliases, two social security cards with two different numbers, and two other forms of identification with different alien registration numbers."

"This rapist had briefly married a woman in Alpharetta, Georgia. We think he may have been married for one purpose, to make the process easier to become a United States citizen," he shared. "Puentes' estranged wife refused to make any further comment."

Was this a monetary transaction between the two, I wondered? Was it legal to marry someone to help them to gain citizenship in the United States?

"The attacker's last arrest was in Cumming, Georgia on multiple charges, including armed burglary, a felony charge in most courtrooms. Unfortunately for you, Puentes struck a plea deal and was released on a misdemeanor charge with probation."

I felt my blood begin to boil. I was angry. I felt the court system had failed me.

"Had the lawyers run his name and prints they would have found his previous charges, including his felonies in the national database. This predator had several aliases. If they had accessed this information, this event would probably not have occurred," the detective concluded.

My big question was, why me? I knew it wasn't my fault. I did nothing to deserve this attack. I understood I was not the cause of his problems, his attacks, or his destiny.

"You will never know the answer to that question," Detective Hennelly said. "All data indicated you were a random target." Even though the police and detectives gathered data from an interview with the ex-wife, and boxed up information from the uncle's car from South

Carolina, nothing pointed to why Puentes chose to attack me.

"Would you like this back?" the detective asked. It was the evidence box containing my Browning Buckmark, the target pistol that saved my life.

"Of course... I would not be here without it. Thank goodness I knew how to shoot and could defend myself; save my life," I said. "The only other outcome for me at that time would have been horrific. I would have been raped, stabbed, and left for dead."

"One last bit of information," the detective said. "As Corporal Ritter mentioned, your case was reviewed and there will be no charges brought against you. You responded to deadly threat with deadly force."

I breathed a sigh of relief.

Somehow, I would have to be at peace with this information. The case was being handed over to the FBI since it involved a person who was not a citizen of these United States.

"I wish I could tell you more but, that is all I have," he said.

I thanked him and he went on his way. It was going to take time for me to make sense of all of this.

CHAPTER 32
Facing the Monster: PTSD

Duluth, Georgia
June 2011 to Present Day

The bathroom shower scene in the movie "Psycho" could not compare to experiencing the real threat. I was cleared of any charges since I protected myself in self-defense, but I was left with the horrific memories. I fought for my life like a soldier at war, only this battle took place in the privacy of my own home.

My military friends were of great support. They all owned guns, hunted, possessed concealed carry permits, and had experience in a war zone defending their lives and the lives of others. My coworkers and colleagues sent emails and phone calls to share their well wishes and love, some sending food, cards, and hugs. Others shared their own personal experiences related to attacks of loved ones by rapists. I was amazed at what people revealed; I thought I was alone with my thoughts and experiences. Their reflections and willingness to confide in me was comforting.

Most of my acquaintances understood my situation, though some questioned and judged my response. Other individuals let their curiosity override their sensitivity to my feelings. Still others found themselves searching their own mind asking the question, "How would I have handled this event?"

A good friend and poet, Charline Payne, wrote a piece for me entitled, *"Phoenix."*

Awesome Bird from the land of the rising sun.

You know not death; you give hope to all.

I, too, was a Phoenix Bird; saved on that day from hell.

I rise from the ashes of my fears –

Transformed with a new courage, confident-

I am well!

My battle would continue against another monster called Post Traumatic Stress Disorder or PTSD. I dealt with the nightmares and lack of sleep, often keeping one eye open for fear of another attack, and the loss of appetite. Every now and again, the memories and flashbacks would flood my brain. I suffered from extraordinarily hypervigilance especially when I was out in the community. I lost trust in people and kept my distance from strangers. Forgetfulness, confusion, and trouble with organization ensued due to emotional overload. Emotions ranged from anger to pain to fear and back again. Taking a shower would never be an experience I would look forward to again, and yet I would face this every day. I installed a hook on the shower wall to hang my firearm.

Counseling helped and time continued to heal my heart and mind. There had been an acceptance of my situation, acceptance for the change in my lifestyle and my relationships, and acceptance in living a new way of life over time. The light began to shine, and laughter and my sense of humor returned. Many memories of horror faded, though they will never be forgotten.

I made several decisions along the way. One was to make a physical move to South Carolina.

Of course, I immediately filed for a South Carolina concealed carry permit, took the written test, and passed the shooting range section with flying colors. The police officer rating this part of the test stated, "Your aim is better than most policemen I know."

I smiled and responded, "Practice makes perfect."

Even though I was making progress in my recovery, I still had many unanswered questions. Had Puentes had a history of this behavior in Cuba, Florida, and other states besides the documented events in Nebraska and Georgia? Why was he allowed to live a life of crime including numerous felonies which included terroristic threats and being in the possession of a firearm within the United States? How is it he never attended a master hearing in almost three years time? Why was he never detained? I felt the community in which I lived was not secure. I would do my research on this topic in time.

CHAPTER 33
News Worthy Headlines

Duluth, Georgia
August 2011 – Present Day

Years have passed. Inquiries continue to come from various agencies including, the Associated Press and the *New York Times*, news talk television, such as the *Sean Hannity Show*, talk radio stations, newspapers and magazines including *Women & Guns*, and programs whose focus are the topics of stalking and survival. The phone would ring after a horrific event had occurred such as the shootings in the elementary school in Newtown, Connecticut.

Emails would be exchanged regarding gun control issues. The reporters and directors of such programing were looking for their spin on newsworthy events and wanted to use my story.

The NRA's monthly magazine called the *American Rifleman* placed my story on page one keeping my identity private. It could be read in The Armed Citizen section of their August issue of 2011.

One afternoon I received a phone call from my brother. He was listening to *The Blaze* radio show, featuring Glenn Beck who had spoken at an *NRA* conference in April 15, 2012.

"Your story is on the radio. Glenn Beck is telling your story," he said.

Glenn Beck had indeed shared stories of various individuals who were able to successfully defend their life with a handgun and survived to tell their story. Applause was heard from the audience when he described how I, in particular, handled the situation and survived due to my knowledge of handguns and self-defense tactics.

Someday I would share my experience. I survived because I was forced to defend my life. I thought quickly and had a plan. I wanted to live. I was not going to leave this world a statistic of sexual assault and/or murder. I had been blessed with a mind that could think under pressure, blessed with a chance to make a difference in the lives of others, and now blessed with a new view of the world. I had a warrior's mindset.

CHAPTER 34
Lessons in Life

Spring, South Carolina
May 2011 to Present Day

What did I learn from this horrific experience? Why do some people survive while others don't? What role does faith play in recovery from emotional bruises? What can I share to make this experience meaningful?

SURVIVAL

Why do some people survive? Why do some individuals bounce back while others don't? What personality allows a person to go through an experience that tests their will and allows them to survive? What is the key to survival? Is it the attitude a person possesses where he or she never loses that will to live? What is situational awareness?

Ben Sherwood, author of *The Survivor's Club,* defined survival as "knowing what is going on around you at any given moment and being able to anticipate danger."[1] He went on to state, "There is a whole lot you can't control and a surprising amount you can. Survival is a lens of how you perceive the world. When faced with a challenge, they observe, they analyze the situation, devise a plan and move decisively. They identify when to stop and when to go."[2]

Everyone is destined to be a survivor. We will all face some life and death crisis or struggle in our lifetime.

---

[1] "The Survivor's Club: The Secrets and Science That Could Save Your Life," Author Ben Sherwood. Grand Central Publishing (2009)16.
[2] "The Survivor's Club: The Secrets and Science That Could Save Your Life," Author Ben Sherwood. Grand Central Publishing (2009)16.

So, what is the definition of a survivor? According to Sherwood, "anyone who faces and overcomes adversity, illness, or physical or emotional trauma; survivors keep going despite setbacks. They don't just exist, they live fully. When knocked down they want to get back up. They accept life probably won't go back to normal so they let go, adapt, and embrace a new normal. The length of time it takes for a person to go through this is different for each person and each event. They have bad days and struggles but they survive too."[3]

In 1992, William Helmreich, a sociologist and professor at City University of New York, studied survival characteristics of those who lived through a horrific experience, the Holocaust. He identified ten characteristics that accounted for their success in life: flexibility, assertiveness, tenacity, optimism, intelligence, distancing ability, group consciousness, the ability to assimilate the knowledge of their survival, the capacity to

---

[3] "The Survivor's Club: The Secrets and Science That Could Save Your Life," Author Ben Sherwood. Grand Central Publishing (2009)175.

find meaning in life, and courage. He noted all of the 170 he interviewed shared some of these qualities and only some of the survivors possessed all. Helmreich stated, "The most critical traits were thinking quickly accompanied by common sense. A basic kind of intelligence – different from book smarts or IQ – enables people to quickly size up situations, break down and analyze problems, and make good decisions."[4]

What does it take to survive? What kind of survivor are you? When you think, "this really isn't happening to me," how do you react? Under duress, they pull themselves together quickly. According to Sherwood, suvivors assess the situation clearly. Their decision-making is sharp and focused. They develop priorities, make plans, and take appropriate action. When faced a real crisis, you discover strengths and abilities you never knew existed.

---

[4] "The Survivor's Club: The Secrets and Science That Could Save Your Life," Author Ben Sherwood. Grand Central Publishing (2009)175.

I was able to stay calm and focused, while in a state of terror. I channeled my fears into action. This occurred after the first few minutes of my attack. I also believed there was a certain amount of divine providence involved.

Sherwood stated, "Survivors aren't fearless, they use fear. They turn it into anger and focus. Survivors have the fighting spirit and willpower."[5] I agree with Sherwood and I know this incident will not define me.

The 80/10/10 rule Sherwood discussed was described as follows: "Eighty percent of your survival depends on your attitude; ten percent on what you know and how you apply it; and ten percent on the tools and equipment you've got to deal with your challenge. The best survival kit is between your ears."[6]

I knew I had joined the club, "The Survivor's Club."

---

[5] "The Survivor's Club: The Secrets and Science That Could Save Your Life," Author Ben Sherwood. Grand Central Publishing (2009)227.
[6] "The Survivor's Club: The Secrets and Science That Could Save Your Life," Author Ben Sherwood. Grand Central Publishing (2009)47.

LUCK OR FAITH

It makes sense that faith plays a part. When you feel weak, it can pump you up. When you are feeling run down, it gives you a boost. If you feel discouraged, it can lift you up. This day, faith gave me strength, guidance, and protection. I think God had a plan for me and gave me the strength and protection to survive this ordeal. I know I asked for assistance from him as I tried to defend and save my life.

I remember staring down the tip of the butcher knife. It was in that instance that I thought I would die. "I can't die today. I have too much to live for. I'm not going out this way. Please God, take care of me, help me, God help me." I would appeal and plead for life. I was not going to be a statistic.

As the situation progressed, and I made every effort to save myself, it seemed like I was experiencing the event in slow motion. The silence was deafening. When I fired the pistol and the light flashed, I remembered asking Jim to make the firearms "hot" so the safety was off. Was this a premonition? Was there a spiritual intervention that took place? Was I just plain lucky? My thoughts transformed from I am going to die to I am going to survive!

Nicholas Rescher of the University of Pittsburgh has written eight books on philosophy, including volumes on the topic of luck. He noted, "The bigger the stakes and the more likely the success, the luckier you are. In short, luck is defined as good or bad fortune acquired unwittingly, by accident or chance."[7] A combination of luck and action is necessary for success. Rescher goes on to report, "Lucky people happen upon chance opportunities. Lucky people listen to their hunches and make good decisions without really knowing why. Lucky people persevere in the face of failure and have an uncanny knack of making their wishes come true. Lucky people have a special ability to turn bad luck into good fortune."[8]

---

[7] "The Survivor's Club: The Secrets and Science That Could Save Your Life," Author Ben Sherwood. Grand Central Publishing (2009)191.
[8] "The Survivor's Club: The Secrets and Science That Could Save Your Life," Author Ben Sherwood. Grand Central Publishing (2009)193.

Did my incident occur as part of a bigger plan? This sexual predator had attacked women repeatedly in his 34 years. He had been caught three times, according to the paper trail in the United States within a 16-month time period. How many other victims had he tortured that were unknown to the legal system and ICE? How many other people prayed for mercy and pleaded for their life? Had he murdered any of his victims? My case was turned over to the FBI since it had become an international case. Therefore, I do not know the answers to these questions.

What I do know is two lives collided, and I survived. For this, I thank God. Thank goodness, I had the ability, and means to protect myself when my government could not.

Need to Know

CHAPTER 35
Questions for ICE and the Legal System

This experience does not have to happen to anyone else. Many questions need to be asked and agencies need to be held accountable for their decisions, action plans, and procedures.

It appears that this convicted felon, known terrorist and sexual predator, with abusive and murderous tendencies was allowed to wreak havoc on the lives of innocent citizens living in their own homes and communities, including my own. The attacker, Israel Perez Puentes, met three of four criteria in order to be detained (a, b and d; c is unknown at this time due to my limited access to records):

a) Two Crimes Involving Moral Turpitude (CIMT) at any time after your admission in the United States;
b) An aggravated felony;
c) A controlled substance offense;
d) A Firearms offense.

Puentes had multiple aliases, alien registration numbers, social security numbers, and residences and had never attended a Master Hearing in the three years he was in the United States. His records include numerous felonies and misdemeanors.

This perpetrator of crimes had a record of scheduled appointments with ICE:

February 5, 2010, Case FAO4843A, Subject has applied for EAD but appears to not have applied for I-485. File to SNA/CCO for review and filing with EOIR, JAJ

April 19, 2010, Case FAO4843A, Next Hearing 08.24.10, Type: Master Hearing

September 9, 2010, Case FAO4843A, Hearing: 03/08/2011, Type: Master Hearing

March 28, 2011, Case PHO7080A, Last/Next Hearing 08/24/10 bp

To deport illegal immigrants, the United States needs travel papers for them, such as a passport. If their native country refuses to issue the necessary papers, the United States cannot deport them. Puentes had such documents, but ICE never placed him into detention for his felonies, including several counts of Terroristic Threats, and the Commission of a Crime while in Possession of a Firearm. His fingerprints were on file.

Our government, the Department of Homeland Security, and the court system set up a system that does not always protect the citizens from violent criminals as seen in this case. The information presented online by the Department of Homeland Security and ICE sounds as if it would be effective. Their strategy should protect the citizens of the United States.

Many questions must be answered in order for the citizens of this country to remain safe from violent criminals that find their way across our borders. Over the past three years, this Administration has undertaken an unprecedented effort to transform the immigration enforcement system into one that focuses on public safety, border security and the integrity of the immigration system. It is said that the Department of Homeland Security continues to focus its enforcement resources on the removal of individuals who pose a danger to national security or a risk to public safety, including individuals convicted of crimes with particular emphasis on violent criminals, felons, and repeat offenders. Of course, this did not happen in my case.

Questions for Our Courts

- Is there a breakdown in communication between the courts and ICE?
- Whose responsibility was it to report this violent criminal's charges to ICE?
- How are the courts in each state educated about the immigration laws?
- Do the court systems feel they will be supported by ICE when they make their reports?
- Do the "sanctuary cities" affect the court's decisions and our public safety?

Questions for the Department of Homeland Security and ICE

- Are there enough funding and resources for the Department of Homeland Security to adequately do its job efficiently and allow ICE to make our country safe?

- How do these agencies prioritize cases for detention that are a violent threat to the public as in this case?

- Is there a "Hot List" maintained by ICE to track criminals such as Puentes? He had committed felonies including two charges of Terroristic Threats and a felony for being in possession of a firearm while in commission of a crime. He had earned a number of felonies and misdemeanors and never sat before an immigration judge for a Master Hearing since his arrival in 2008. His Master Hearings were scheduled for the following dates: 2/5/10, 4/19/2010, 09/09/2010, and 3/28/2011. He was apparently never report to ICE or tracked.

- Does ICE and the Department of Homeland Security need to increase detention centers for violent criminals that are slow to be deported or in countries such as Cuba that have no extradition treaties with the United States even if the individual has "authentic" travel documents?

Sanctuary Cities

Across the U.S., there are over 300 cities, counties, and states that are considered "sanctuary cities." These jurisdiction protect criminal aliens from deportation by refusing to comply with ICE detainers or otherwise impede open communication and information exchanges between their employees or officers and federal immigration agents.

In this case, Puentes had been found guilty in cases where the cities were located incounties which were on the "sanctuary cities" list.

- Why do criminal aliens involved in criminal cases have different consequences for their actions than an individual who is a citizen of the United States in these cities?
- Can the state governments reverse "sanctuary city" laws?

APPENDIX I
Mission Statement - ICE

The Department of Homeland Security shares the U.S. Immigration and Customs Reinforcement mission statement on their websites. It states:

"The mission is to identify, arrest, and remove aliens who present a danger to national security or are a risk to public safety, as well as those who enter the United States illegally or otherwise undermine the integrity of our immigration laws and our border control efforts. Enforcement and Removal Operations (ERO) upholds America's immigration laws at, within and beyond our borders through efficient enforcement and removal operations."

Further information from their website related to how ERO upholds laws, includes the following:

ERO enforces the nation's immigration laws in a fair and effective manner. It identifies and apprehends removable aliens, detains these individuals when necessary and removes illegal aliens from the United States.

ERO prioritizes the apprehension, arrest and removal of convicted criminals, those who pose a threat to national security, fugitives and recent border entrants. Individuals seeking asylum also work with ERO.

ERO transports removable aliens from point to point, manages aliens in custody or in an alternative to detention program, provides access to legal resources and representatives of advocacy groups and removes individuals from the United States who have been ordered to be deported.

According to the government's website, ICE has specific removal policies in place.

FY 2014 ICE Immigration Removals
In addition to its criminal investigative responsibilities, ICE shares responsibility for

enforcing the nation's civil immigration laws with U.S. Customs and Border Protection (CBP) and U.S. Citizenship and Immigration Services (USCIS). ICE's role in the immigration enforcement system is focused on two primary missions:

(1) The identification and apprehension of criminal aliens and other removable individuals located in the United States; and

(2) The detention and removal of those individuals apprehended in the interior of the U.S., as well as those apprehended by CBP officers and agents patrolling our nation's borders.

In executing these responsibilities, ICE has prioritized its limited resources on the identification and removal of criminal aliens and those apprehended at the border while attempting to unlawfully enter the United States. This report provides an overview of ICE Fiscal Year (FY) 2014 civil immigration enforcement and removal operations.

Website Source - http://www.ice.gov/ero

This report summarizes U.S. Immigration and Customs Enforcement's (ICE) Fiscal Year (FY) 2014 civil immigration enforcement and removal operations.

ICE shares responsibility for enforcing the Nation's civil immigration laws with U.S. Customs and Border Protection (CBP) and U.S. Citizenship and Immigration Services (USCIS). In executing its enforcement duties, ICE focuses on two core missions: (1) identifying and apprehending public safety threats—including criminal aliens and national security targets—and other removable individuals within the United States; and (2) detaining and removing individuals apprehended by ICE and CBP officers and agents patrolling our Nation's borders.

Each year, ICE immigration enforcement is impacted by operational factors, including the size of the removable population found in the interior and encountered at the border by CBP, appropriated resources, fluctuating migration patterns, and the legal authorities that govern ICE's activities. In 2014, each of these factors affected ICE operations and contributed to the number of ICE's FY 2014 removals, which was 315,943, down from 368,644 in FY 2013. This report sets forth and analyzes ICE's FY 2014 immigration enforcement statistics:

In FY 2014, ICE reports the statistics regarding removal of criminals:

ICE conducted 315,943 removals.

ICE conducted 102,224 removals of individuals apprehended in the interior of the United States.

86,923 (85 percent) of all interior removals involved individuals previously convicted of a crime.

ICE conducted 213,719 removals of individuals apprehended while attempting to unlawfully enter the United States.[9]

56 percent of all ICE removals, or 177,960, involved individuals who were previously convicted of a crime.

ICE apprehended and removed 86,923 criminals from the interior of the U.S.

ICE removed 91,037 criminals apprehended while attempting to unlawfully enter the United States.

98 percent of all ICE FY 2014 removals, or 309,477, clearly met one or more of ICE's

---

[9] Approximately 96 percent of these individuals were apprehended by CBP Border Patrol agents and then processed, detained, and removed by ICE. The remaining individuals were apprehended by CBP officers at ports of entry.

stated civil immigration enforcement priorities.[10]

Of the 137,983 individuals removed who had no criminal conviction, 89 percent, or 122,682, were apprehended at or near the border while attempting to unlawfully enter the country.[11]

The leading countries of origin for removals were Mexico, Guatemala, Honduras, and El Salvador.

2,802 individuals removed by ICE were classified as suspected or confirmed gang members.[12]

Website Source - http://www.ice.gov/removal-statistics

---

[10] As defined in the March 2011 ICE Memorandum: Civil Immigration Enforcement: Priorities for the Apprehension, Detention, and Removal of Aliens.

[11] ICE defines criminality via a recorded criminal conviction obtained by ICE officers and agents from certified criminal history repositories. These individuals include recent border crossers, immigration fugitives, and repeat immigration violators.

[12] Gang affiliation is documented as part of the intake process in the Risk Classification Assessment (RCA).

Definitions of Key Terms

Border Removal: An individual removed by ICE who is apprehended while attempting to illicitly enter the United States at or between the ports of entry by a CBP officer or agent. These individuals are also referred to as recent border crossers.

Criminal Offender: An individual convicted in the United States for one or more criminal offenses. This does not include civil traffic offenses.

Immigration Fugitives: An individual who has failed to leave the United States based upon a final order of removal, deportation or exclusion, or who has failed to report to ICE after receiving notice to do so.

Interior Removal: An individual removed by ICE who is identified or apprehended in the United States by an ICE officer or agent. This category excludes those apprehended at the immediate border while attempting to unlawfully enter the United States.

Other Removable Alien: An individual who is not confirmed to be a convicted criminal, recent border crosser or fall under another ICE civil enforcement priority category. This category may include individuals removed on national security grounds or for general immigration violations.

Previously Removed Alien: An individual previously removed or returned who has re-entered the country illegally again.

Reinstatement of Final Removal Order: The removal of an alien based on the reinstatement of a prior removal order, where the alien departed the United States under an order of removal and illegally reentered the United States [INA § 241(a)(5)]. The alien may be removed without a hearing before an immigration court.

Removal: The compulsory and confirmed movement of an inadmissible or deportable alien out of the United States based on an order of removal. An individual who is removed may have administrative or criminal consequences placed on subsequent reentry owing to the fact of the removal.

Website Source: http://www.ice.gov/removal-statistics.

How can we help our citizens be safer in our own country? What will it take for our court system to understand what needs to happen for ICE to do the job of detaining criminals that break our laws? What information does ICE provide to create more Secure Communities?

The following information is available for the public to view on http://www.ice.gov/secure-communities. It sounds like a great plan, but how can the public be sure it will be implemented as it did not happen in the cases reported in this book?

Secure Communities

The highest priority of any law enforcement agency is to protect the communities it serves. When it comes to enforcing our nation's immigration laws, U.S. Immigration and Customs Enforcement (ICE) focused its limited resources on those who have been arrested for breaking criminal laws.

ICE prioritizes the removal of criminal aliens, those who pose a threat to public safety, and repeat immigration violators.

Secure Communities is a simple and common sense way to carry out ICE's priorities. It uses an already-existing federal information-sharing partnership between ICE and the

Federal Bureau of Investigation (FBI) that helps to identify criminal aliens without imposing new or additional requirements on state and local law enforcement. For decades, local jurisdictions have shared the fingerprints of individuals who are arrested or booked into custody with the FBI to see if they have a criminal record. Under Secure Communities, the FBI automatically sends the fingerprints to DHS to check against its immigration databases. If these checks reveal that an individual is unlawfully present in the United States or otherwise removable due to a criminal conviction, ICE takes enforcement action – prioritizing the removal of individuals who present the most significant threats to public safety as determined by the severity of their crime, their criminal history, and other factors – as well as those who have repeatedly violated immigration laws.

Secure Communities imposes no new or additional requirements on state and local law enforcement. The federal government, not the state or local law enforcement agency, determines what immigration enforcement action, if any, is appropriate.

Only federal DHS officers make immigration enforcement decisions, and they do so only after an individual is arrested for a criminal violation of local, state, or federal law, separate and apart from any violations of immigration law.

The Basics

More than 283,000 convicted criminal aliens have been removed as a result of Secure Communities interoperability, by which the FBI automatically sends fingerprints of anyone arrested or booked by police for a state or local criminal offense to DHS to check against its immigration and enforcement records so that ICE can determine whether that person is a criminal alien or falls under ICE's civil immigration enforcement priorities.

Since its inception in 2008 with 14 jurisdictions, Secure Communities has expanded to all 3,181 jurisdictions within 50 states, the District of Columbia, and five (5) U.S. Territories. Full implementation was completed on January 22, 2013.

How Does Secure Communities Work?

ICE receives annual appropriations from Congress sufficient to remove a limited number of the more than 10 lawful statuses or is removable because of a criminal conviction.

Given this reality, ICE must set sensible priorities.

Under the Obama administration, ICE has set clear and common sense priorities for immigration enforcement focused on identifying and removing those aliens with criminal convictions. In addition to criminal aliens, ICE focuses on recent illegal entrants, repeat violators who game the immigration system, those who fail to appear at immigration hearings, and fugitives who have already been ordered removed by an immigration judge.

These priorities have led to significant results. In fiscal year 2013, ICE's prioritized, targeted enforcement resulted in the removal of more than 368,000 aliens, of which 98 percent fell into one of ICE's stated civil immigration enforcement priorities.

The Process: Secure Communities: From Arrest to Release or Removal

When state and local law enforcement arrest or book someone into custody for a violation of a criminal offense, they generally fingerprint the person. After fingerprints are taken at the jail, the state and local authorities electronically submit the fingerprints to the Federal Bureau of Investigation (FBI). This data is then stored in the FBI's criminal databases. After running the fingerprints against those databases, the FBI sends the state and local authorities a record of the person's criminal history.

With Secure Communities, once the FBI checks the fingerprints, the FBI automatically sends them to DHS, so that U.S. Immigration and Customs Enforcement (ICE) can determine if that person is also subject to removal (deportation). This change, whereby the fingerprints are sent to DHS in addition to the FBI, fulfills a 2002 Congressional mandate for the FBI to share information with ICE, and is consistent with a 2008 federal law that instructs ICE to identify criminal aliens for removal. Secure Communities does not require any changes in the procedures of local law enforcement agencies or jails.

If the person has been previously encountered and fingerprinted by an immigration official and there is a digitized record, then the immigration database will register a "match." ICE then reviews other databases to determine whether the person is here illegally or is otherwise removable.

In cases where the person appears from these checks to be removable, ICE generally issues a detainer on the person, requesting that the state or local jail facility hold the individual up to an extra 48 hours (excluding weekends) to allow for an interview of the person. Following the interview, ICE decides whether to seek the person's removal.

In making these decisions, ICE considers a number of factors, including the person's criminal history, immigration history (such as whether the person was previously deported or has an outstanding removal order from an immigration judge), family ties, duration of stay in the U.S., significant medical issues, and other circumstances. In many instances involving lower-level criminals or people who are not convicts, re-entrants, or fugitives, ICE offers the person the option of voluntary return. A voluntary return allows the person to enter the U.S. lawfully in the future.

When someone goes into immigration proceedings, the court process is run independent of the state criminal justice system. As a result, illegal immigrants can be removed before the criminal case is complete. There is a variety of reasons that the local arrest may not result in a criminal conviction. However, all of those removed are guilty of an immigration violation, and removed pursuant to the Immigration and Nationality Act.

What went wrong in the Puentes case? Why were the rules and regulations not followed? What are the priorities set forth by ICE? According to their website, ICE has set certain priorities.

Advancing ICE's Priorities

Enforcing America's immigration laws is a federal responsibility. Under the Homeland Security Act of 2002, this responsibility falls to DHS, specifically U.S. Immigration and Customs Enforcement (ICE).

Since 2008, Congress has expanded ICE's immigration enforcement obligations – directing ICE to create a strategy to identify criminal aliens and prioritize them for removal.

In light of this direction and the fact that ICE receives limited resources, ICE must prioritize which of the estimated 10 million illegal immigrants in the United States and other removable aliens to pursue. In a memo issued by ICE Director John Morton in June 2010, ICE outlined the way it prioritizes removals. Specifically, ICE prioritizes the removal of those who pose a danger to national security or public safety, repeat violators who game the immigration system, those who fail to appear at immigration hearings, and fugitives who have already been ordered removed by an immigration judge. Because the administration is committed to using immigration enforcement resources in the way most beneficial to public safety, the primary focus is on convicted criminals, with a priority on aggravated felons.

As a result, record numbers of criminal aliens have been removed, with Secure Communities playing a key role in ICE's ability to fulfill this public safety priority. Between October 2008 and October 2011, the number of convicted criminals that ICE removed from the United States increased 89 percent, while the number of aliens removed without criminal convictions dropped by 29 percent. These trends are due in significant part to the implementation and expansion of Secure Communities. While Secure Communities is only responsible for a limited percentage of ICE's total removals and returns, it has helped ICE identify a more significant percentage of the convicted criminals that ICE removes or returns.

Over time, the percentage of serious offenders removed through Secure Communities will continue to increase, as those convicted of misdemeanors will decrease. This reflects the fact that people who commit more serious crimes serve longer sentences and consequently take longer to come into ICE custody. Since Secure Communities was first activated in October 2008, the percentage of misdemeanant removals has decreased from 40 percent of all removals in fiscal year 2009 to 29 percent of all removals following identification through Secure Communities in fiscal year 2011.

Civil Rights and Civil Liberties

Secure Communities reduces opportunities for racial or ethnic profiling because ALL people booked into jails are fingerprinted. U.S. Immigration and Customs Enforcement (ICE) and DHS' *Office for Civil Rights and Civil Liberties* (CRCL) are currently implementing additional safeguards to further protect Secure Communities from those who may seek to use it improperly.

Several initiatives to achieve these goals are underway:

In order to identify jurisdictions that may be making improper arrests that could result in identification of aliens through Secure Communities, ICE and CRCL have retained a leading statistician who is examining data for each jurisdiction where Secure Communities is activated, comparing data for aliens identified by Secure Communities to relevant arrest-rate data, and identifying any indications of racial profiling. Statistical outliers will be subject to an in-depth analysis. This analysis will take place four times per year to ensure consistent monitoring, and the assessments will be shared quarterly with the Department of Justice. Statistical outliers in local jurisdictions will be subject to an in-depth analysis and DHS and ICE will take appropriate steps to resolve any issues. View the *Overview of Quarterly Statistical Monitoring* (PDF | 260 KB).

To prevent and address possible abuses of Secure Communities, ICE and CRCL are working together to develop a new training program for state and local law enforcement agencies in jurisdictions where Secure Communities is activated. These training materials are designed to reduce confusion regarding Secure Communities and help ensure that it is not misused. Four video briefings, with supporting materials, have already been released, with more to follow throughout calendar year 2012.

ICE has revised the detainer form ICE submits to local jurisdictions to emphasize the longstanding guidance that state and local authorities are not to detain an individual for more than 48 hours. The form also requires local law enforcement to provide arrestees with a copy, which has a number to call if they believe their civil rights have been violated.

Still more questions arise. Does ICE have enough resources to protect the citizens of the United States? Does a lack of funding then cause a ripple effect of issues that are detrimental to the safety of our citizens in the United States? When will the government take control of a system that is failing the people?

ICE posted the following responses by various secure community agencies and individuals in May of 2011.

Secure Communities

Secure Communities is U.S. Immigration and Customs Enforcement's (ICE) comprehensive strategy to improve and modernize the identification and removal of convicted criminal aliens from the United States. As part of this strategy, ICE is leveraging a federal biometric information sharing capability to quickly and accurately identify aliens in law enforcement custody. Once identified, ICE prioritizes convicted criminal aliens for removal from the United States. ICE is also conducting modeling and analysis of the current criminal alien enforcement process to ensure the right people, resources and processes are in place to make immigration enforcement more efficient and effective.

The National Sheriffs' Association, Major County Sheriffs' Association, the New York State Sheriffs' Association and the New York State Association of Chiefs of Police have all issued formal statements in support of Secure Communities.

Senator Orrin Hatch, U.S. Senate, Utah Finance, Judiciary & Intelligence Committees

"By tapping innovative technology and sharing information between law enforcement agencies, Utah now has one more tool in its arsenal to protect our streets from criminal activity. Today's announcement (activation of IDENT/IAFIS interoperability) is certainly a step in the right direction, and in the near future, we hope to have even more Utah counties participate in the program."[13]

Sheriff Larry Campbell, Leon County Sheriff's Office, Florida

---

13 "Secure Communities expands to Utah," ICE press release, www.ice.gov, March 31, 2010.

"Secure Communities is about information sharing and will reduce allegations of racial and ethnic profiling. This is not a random sampling of fingerprints submitted by officers on the street. The fingerprints of every person arrested and booked into the Leon County Jail will be checked against immigration records. (...) The use of Secure Communities means criminal aliens can no longer hide behind a long list of aliases."[14]

Sheriff Mike Wade, Henrico County Sheriff's Office, Virginia

"Secure Communities enables us to get a more accurate picture of who we have in custody so we can best manage our time and resources."[15]

Sheriff Matt McCaffrey, Sonoma County Sheriff's Office, California

"This is a common-sense approach: Everyone who gets arrested gets checked for

---

14 "Leon County Sheriff's Office Joins ICE Secure Communities Initiative to Enhance Identification and Removal of Criminal Aliens," Leon County, Florida, Sheriff's Office, April 26, 2010.

[15] "Additional Virginia jurisdictions to benefit from ICE strategy to enhance the identification, removal of criminal aliens," Ethiopian Review, April 24, 2010.

immigration status. In this case, they're already in the system for entering into the country illegally or for having a record. There are individuals in the country illegally and they're re-offending. Now, they're not going to be re-offending in Sonoma County."[16]

Representative Henry Cuellar, Texas, Ranking Member, U.S. House of Representatives Homeland Security Subcommittee on Border, Maritime and Global Counterterrorism

"Criminal elements are everywhere, and one of our duties is to ensure our residents are protected. This is important because it provides a process for getting criminal aliens off of our streets."[17]

Washington Post Editorial Board

"Secure Communities...authorizes an immigration check only if someone has been charged. Even then, confirmation of illegal status rightly does not automatically trigger deportation. Immigration and Customs Enforcement (ICE) focuses on those with

---

[16] "New jail program targets illegal immigrants," Julie Tolland, The Press Democrat, March 2, 2010.
[17] "County to share fingerprints with 'ICE,'" Ron Maloney, The Gazette-Enterprise, June 9, 2010.

convictions for serious felonies including violent crimes." [18]

Captain Gerald Cooper, Los Angeles County Sheriff's Department, California

"It helps people from falling through the cracks, (...) it helps prevent us from allowing very dangerous people from getting out of custody and back into the community when they should be interviewed by ICE and potentially held by ICE."[19]

Chief Sid Fuller, Farmers Branch Police Department, Texas

"Secure Communities is a great example of using interagency cooperation and technology to fight crime."[20]

Sheriff Jim Winder, Salt Lake County Sheriff's Office, Utah

"This program, Secure Communities, strikes, in my opinion, the perfect balance between the

---

[18] "How to improve an immigration status check", Washington Post, March 20, 2011.
[19] "ICE officers using program to control criminal immigrants," San Bernardino Sun, April 13, 2010.
[20] "New program enhances identifying and deporting criminal aliens in more north Texas law enforcement agencies," Kaufman Herald, February 25, 2009.

need to maintain individual civil rights and the identification of people that have done criminal acts and will eventually be held accountable."[21]

Sgt. J.D. Nelson, Public Information Officer, Alameda County Sheriff's Office, California

"We just submit our prints like we always have. It doesn't impact us or our workload one way or another."[22]

Sheriff Lee Baca, Los Angeles County Sheriff's Office, California

"Secure Communities deters some illegal immigrants from committing crimes. People are more cautious because the program is in existence."[23]

Sheriff Rick Jones, Butler County Sheriff's Office, Ohio

"Before, we had people that were in our jail that had several aliases. We didn't know who they were. Sometimes they have 12 names,

---

[21] "Utah Jails Using Federal Database To Identify Illegal Immigrants, KSL–TV (Salt Lake City), April 1, 2010.

[22] "States Rebel Over Deportations", The Wall Street Journal, May 14, 2011.

[23] "On the Record with Greta Van Susteren: Secure Communities: Fingerprint for Rounding Up Illegal Immigrants?," FOX News, July 27, 2010.

different Social Security numbers. They can't fudge or fake that fingerprint. That fingerprint detects—tells us who they are, tells ICE who they are. And Secure Communities is actually here to deport and make arrests on criminal aliens, people who have come here illegally and have committed a crime or have a criminal history."[24]

Lt. Basilio "Sonny" Cachuela, Jr., Public Information Officer Fairfax County Sheriff's Office, VA

"There are no community divisions being created with this program...We are not going out into the community seeking illegal aliens. No one is sought out, and no one is fingerprinted other than criminals processed into our jail."[25]

Representative David Price, North Carolina, Ranking Member U.S. House of Representatives Appropriations Subcommittee on Homeland Security

"Secure Communities draws that bright line between the federal role and the local role in

---

[24] "Sheriff Defends Fairfax County's Partnership with Federal Agency", Fairfax Times, December 7, 2010.
[25] "Utah Jails Using Federal Database To Identify Illegal Immigrants, KSL–TV (Salt Lake City), April 1, 2010.

immigration enforcement....I believe it can accomplish the task more efficiently to identify and remove dangerous criminals from our communities, which I think we very widely agree should be the main priority of immigration enforcement."[26]

Website Source - What Others Are Saying...About Secure Communities - http://www.ice.gov/doclib/secure-communities/pdf/what-others-say.pdf, 2006/11

This data sounds solid, so why are the citizens of the United States not safe?

I can only make the following conclusions. It is clear that Israel Perez Puentes was not prosecuted to the full extent of the law. He was a "criminal offender," an individual convicted in the United States for one or more criminal offenses. The Border Patrol and the legal system had in effect allowed this individual to live in the United States by allowing the delay the Master Hearing for several years. The courts failed to

---

[26] 157 Cong. Rec. H3947-48 (daily ed. June 2, 2011) (statement of Rep. David Price).

report him to ICE and the Department of Homeland Security. The system failed to protect me and at least two other women according to records obtained. Puentes, a multi-state offender who spent only 67 days in jails for multiple felonies including charges of terroristic threats and felony possession of a firearm while in commission of a crime with multiple misdemeanors, was not detained or placed on a deportation list, but allowed to roam free to commit egregious and violent acts of terrorism.

What should happen next? Did the Secure Communities fail to come into play with this case? Did his residences in various "sanctuary cities" affect the outcome of his court cases? What change in policies and procedures should the citizens of the United States expect from ICE, the Department of Homeland Security, and the judicial systems?

We need to look to our government to develop a solid policy that will protect its citizens.

APPENDIX II
Tips for Home Defense and Self-Protection

There are many ways to live more safely, especially if you live alone. I will cover tips for home defense, self-protection, the choice of handgun as a weapon for self-defense, what to do if you are raped or robbed, driving issues, and your right to defend yourself. I also included a list of support resources for victims and their family members.

Home Defense

How can you make your home safe from unwanted intruders? Here are a few helpful tips:

1. If you can afford it, get a security alarm system. If not, at least place signs outside of your house. You can purchase inexpensive signs and fake alarm decals at most hardware stores.
2. Turn webcams into your security system.
3. Place a "Beware of Dog" sign with a bowl and heavy chain in your back yard or on your porch if you do not own a dog.
4. If you love dogs, consider getting one. They have great ears and can be the first line of protection.
5. Use double bolt locks on solid wood or steel doors.
6. For sliding glass doors, drill hole for extended pin insert in metal frames of two glass doors. Cut a dowel or broomstick to place along the base of the door to prevent it from being forced open. Be sure the latch works.
7. Maintain the shrubbery around house; keep it lower than the windowsill. You do not want would be robbers hiding behind them. Keep your lawn maintained so your house has that "lived in" look.

8. Install motion-detection security lights and lights at door entrances to your home. Check them periodically to be sure each light illuminates.

9. Be sure window locks are in working condition. Install extra window locks so they cannot be jimmied open. You can also cut a dowel the length of window from top of sill to top of window. This would be an inexpensive fix too.

10. Purchase magnetic contact alarms for a few dollars for your windows and doors. The sensors release a siren sound when contact between the two pieces is separated.

11. Use blinds or drapes to give you privacy. This is important when you are not home and in the evening.

12. Do not leave boxes outside your home especially around holidays. You do not want everyone to know you just purchased a 50-inch plasma TV.

13. Check mail daily and do not leave outgoing mail in the box to be picked up by the mail carrier.

14. You may even want to consider a post office box if you don't want important papers, bills and other mail coming to your house. Robbers often go through the mailbox to review identification information.

15. Do not let flyers pile up outside your front door. Cancel newspaper delivery while you are away. Have neighbors check your mailbox.

16. Keep a number on your house so police and firefighters can find it easily but do not have a sign made with your name on it, i.e. The Jones.

17. Talk with your neighbors. Keep an eye out for each other.

18. A fenced in yard may deter prowlers.

19. Leave lights on timers throughout the day and night. Switch up the times now and again.

20. Do you have an interior bathroom? If so, you may use that one in early mornings now and then. This will switch up how lighting is viewed from the outside.

21. Do not open doors for strangers. Do offer to call 911 for them if need be.
22. Consider a separate line or cellular security device.
23. Keep doors locked at all times. Many break-ins are now occurring during the day.
24. Do not leave a ladder out in your backyard.
25. Build a secret hiding place for valuables.
26. If you are concerned about activity outside your home or think someone is trying to break in, use your car remote and press the panic button. The sound of honking horns will draw attention to your home and the intruder may decide to flee.
27. Do not leave status updates on your vacation on social media. Prowlers will know you are away.

Self-Protection Options

1. Be aware of your surroundings.
2. Have your keys ready when entering and exiting your home or car.
3. Do carry pepper spray, a Taser, or weapon. You will need to have instruction on how

to use these should you choose to carry them.

4. Have access to a claw hammer or hornet spray that shoots 15 feet so you can defend yourself at home in a moment's notice.

5. If you are leaving work, or a mall, a hospital or an area that is not well lit, ask someone to escort you to your car.

6. Fan keys between fingers as you walk to car. The keys can be used as a weapon.

7. Be sure to keep purse over your shoulder so it cannot be easily removed. If your purse is grabbed, let it go. Better to be safe than sorry.

8. Be aware of your parking space; look under the car and on both sides as you approach it. Unlock and lock doors as soon as you get in.

9. At the gas pump, remove keys and lock doors. Make eye contact with people around you.

10. Keep your car in good running condition.

11. If approached and threatened, yell, scream, kick, shout "Fire, fire," anything to draw attention to your situation, and drop to the

ground. It will make it harder for you to be moved.

12. Take a self-defense course that can teach you lessons for offense rather than defense: i.e. kick to the groin, chop to the throat or upward hit to the nose. Criminals prefer to attack easy targets. If you are going to fight back, know how to.

13. Avoid date rape scenarios by always letting friends know where you are and do not let your drinks go unattended. Someone could administer a date rape drug in your absence. Do not accept drinks from strangers. If you suspect you have been drugged or see a friend exhibiting the symptoms, call an ambulance. You or your friend could easily pass out, fall and end up in a coma or dead. If you feel you have been a victim of a crime such as rape, preserve the evidence of DNA and report the crime. If you do not report, others may suffer the same fate.

14. Program 911 into your cell phone.

15. Exit the car after closing your garage door; this is the safety of having a garage door opener readily available.
16. Always drive with your doors locked.
17. If possible, switch up where you park at work or school.
18. Plan the safest route to your destination and use it. Use well-lit and busy streets and avoid passing vacant lots or construction sites.
19. Walk facing traffic so you can see approaching cars.
20. Do not run with headphones; you will not hear anyone who could approach from behind.
21. Do not flaunt jewelry.
22. Do not overburden yourself with packages and groceries. Get help from the store.
23. Bring emergency cash for a cab or bus fare.
24. If you suspect you are being followed while on foot, cross the street and head to a well-lit populated area. Scream if you need to. You can always take down the license plate number if you suspect you are being followed.

The Handgun for Self-Defense

If you decide to purchase a gun, you will need to ask yourself some questions. Should that awful moment ever arise, could you use your gun on an attacker to defend your life or the life of a family member? You will have to answer this question for yourself. Would you be able to live with the emotional scars that may follow and perhaps even the social and legal ramifications? Can you spiritually reconcile this question with your faith? In all honesty, if you are not willing to explore these questions and cannot answer "yes" to them and perhaps others that arise for you personally, you are not ready and should not own a gun. The question and answer of whether or not you could use a gun is a complex and very personal one.

Some time should be taken to think through potential worst-case scenarios and how you would react. Take the time to think about what your options are. This process also helps to create a series of plans of action that under great stress, you can default to and lower the risk of making poor decisions and perhaps injuring or killing yourself or an innocent bystander.

This important process needs to be done in depth and detail. The news on any given day can provide the scenes to provoke this exercise. Imagine yourself in these situations and explore what you would have done. What could you have done differently?

Once you have gone through this exercise in different situations, such as an attack in a parking lot, a home invasion, carjacking, sexual/violent attack or others, the next series of questions is what tools do you need and how do you train to effectively and safely use them?

The legal issues of using your gun are complex and different from state-to-state. Your local laws must be explored as to fully understand your rights and the laws that govern gun ownership and use. Explore the local and state laws governing the use of "lethal deadly force." If someone breaks into your home, is it legal to use a gun and shoot him or her even if he or she is not visibly armed? If someone attacks you in public, do you have a duty to retreat? Under what circumstances can you legally display your gun? Under what circumstances can you legally use your gun? Are there places where you cannot carry a gun? Can you travel across state lines with your gun? These are just a few of the questions you want to answer as you make the decision to use and own a gun. As you can see, the legal issues of using a gun are very complex and demand your further study.

Gun safety includes use and storage. Sign up for training from an arms instructor. Remember, you must practice, practice, and practice. Get comfortable with all aspects of owning and using a gun from loading, to unloading, and firing to cleaning. Practice gun safety. Do you want to carry the weapon outside your home? Investigate a carry permit for your state. Learn the rules and take the tests that are involved. Continue to practice. Know your rights. If you have questions, seek an answer from the professional. Read more on Women and Guns website:
http://thewellarmedwoman.com/women-and-guns.

What If You Are Raped?

- Try not to panic. Look at your attacker carefully so you can describe him to the police. Try to remember things like age, height, weight, complexion, body build, clothing, hair, scars, and voice.
- Try stalling for time, distracting the attacker and fleeing to a safe place, screaming to attract attention, or fighting back. By acting crazy, you may discourage him. Trust your instincts.
- If a weapon is present, then trust your judgment and submit if you must. The most important point is that you trust yourself to know what is best. Every situation is different. Each person and how they react is different.
- If you choose to resist, get mad, not scared. Use your anger to give you strength. Rapists depend on fear and may be discouraged by aggressiveness, yelling. If you choose to fight to win, never give up.

Stalking has become one of the most dreaded crimes against women in recent years.

According to a 2013 study conducted by the government office, the Bureau of Justice Statistics, one woman in 12 will be stalked during her lifetime. This figure is startling when compared to the fact that 1 in 3,000 will be raped, based on current FBI statistics. According to the 2013 FBI and the Bureau of Justice Statistics, an estimated 14 in every 1,000 persons age 18 or older were victims of stalking during a 12-month period.

If you find yourself in a situation where you have been raped, try to remember the following steps.

1. Report the incident immediately to the police. Do not call family. Call the police.
2. Secure any DNA as evidence (clothes, bed sheets) and place in bag or container. Try not to disturb the actual location of the incident until the crime lab arrives. If possible, do not allow EMT or police officers to destroy evidence by accident.
3. Do not bathe or clean your house before authorities arrive.

4. If it is safe to do so, stay at the scene. You will be able to identify the exact place the attack occurred.

5. Try to put shame and embarrassment aside and focus strictly on the details. You may feel a range of emotions from shock, anger, to depression but try to be prepared to share the facts as you know them. If you feel uncomfortable with what a policeman or detective may be expressing, ask for a female police officer or detective to come to your assistance.

6. If you have to return for questioning, to speak to authorities, dress appropriately and speak with confidence. Arrive on time and do not hesitate to ask for assistance with the district attorney if you do not have an attorney to speak on your behalf.

7. Do not contact the suspect's attorney, private detectives or news media without approval of the authorities. Anything you say to them may be recorded or documented and they may distort or embellish what you have said to them. This can be used in court against you. Be smart.

8. If you have to go to court, dress appropriately, look straight at the jurors, make eye contact. Talk to the jury as if you were addressing a group of friends. Remember, they want to believe you because why would you put yourself through such agony and distress? If you find yourself angry, hold any smart remarks or belligerence until after court.

9. Stand up for your rights; ask for assistance from the attorney.

10. Be sure to receive the professional counseling you may need to sort through your experience. This will take time and that is okay.

What if Someone Tries to Rob You?

- Remain calm. Try not to panic, and try not to show any signs of anger or confusion.
- If the attacker is only after your purse, do not resist. Let it go.
- Make a conscious effort to get an accurate description of your robber.
- Call the police immediately, identifying yourself and your location.

- If you have been traumatized, contact victims assistance for help processing the event.

Driving Issues

We all try to keep our vehicles in good running condition, but there may be a time your car acts up or breaks down. What should you do? If you have a cell phone, contact 911, the HERO unit, or AAA. Keep your windows rolled up and the doors locked while you wait. You may need to indicate you need assistance by raising the hood, using flares or tying a white cloth to your door handle.

In regards to parking, always choose a well-lit area. Lock your car doors and be alert, especially in underground garage parking areas. Ask someone to escort you if you are afraid of being approached.

If you suspect you are being followed, drive to the nearest police department or fire station, open gas station or well-lit residence where you can call police. Try to get the license tag number and description. If there are no safe areas, honk your horn repeatedly and turn on your emergency flashers.

Avoiding dangerous situations is your best bet, but if you find yourself in a precarious and dangerous situation, defending yourself is the most moral and ethical course of action.

APPENDIX III
Self-Help and Support Resources

Counseling and support for women and men who have been attacked can be a stepping-stone to a healthy lifestyle. There are many organizations and support groups to fit each person's needs. Sources can be researched online, through your local police or sheriff's office, or the district attorney. Here is a list of a few organizations that may help you find the support you need:

1. National Center for Victims of Crime
   http://www.victimsofcrime.org/
2. National Organization of Victims Assistance
   http://www.try-nova.org/

3. National Organization of Parents of Murdered Children
   http://www.www.pomc.com/

4. The Stalking Victims Society
   http://stalkingvictims.com/

Other national groups:

5. Broken Spirits
   info@brokenspirits.com

6. National Coalition Against Domestic Violence
   http://www.ncadv.org/

7. National Domestic Violence Hotline
   800-799-SAFE (7233)

8. Partners of Assault Survivors
   http://www.geocities.ws/rapecrisisinformation/Partners.htm

9. Rape, Abuse & Incest National Network (RAINN)
   https://www.rainn.org/

10. SOAR – Speaking Out Against Rape
    http://soar99.org/blog/

APPENDIX IV
More About Stalking

According to the Supplemental Victimization Survey (SVS), individuals are classified as stalking victims if they experienced at least one of these behaviors on at least two separate occasions. In addition, the individuals must have feared for their safety or that of a family member as a result of the course of conduct, or have experienced additional threatening behaviors that would cause a reasonable person to feel fear.

The SVS measures stalking behaviors as:

- making unwanted phone calls
- sending unsolicited or unwanted letters or e-mails
- following or spying on the victim
- showing up at places without a legitimate reason

- waiting at places for the victim
- leaving unwanted items, presents, or flowers
- posting information or spreading rumors about the victim on the internet, in a public place, or by word of mouth

Stalking Laws

The federal government, all 50 states, the District of Columbia, and U.S. Territories have enacted criminal laws to address stalking. The legal definition for stalking varies across jurisdictions:

- State laws vary regarding the element of victim fear and emotional distress, as well as the requisite intent of the stalker.
- Some state laws specify that the victim must have been frightened by the stalking, while others require only that the stalking behavior would have caused a reasonable person to experience fear.
- States vary regarding what level of fear is required.
- Some state laws require prosecutors to establish fear of death or serious bodily

harm, while others require only that prosecutors establish that the victim suffered emotional distress.

- Interstate stalking is defined by federal law 18 U.S.C. § 2261A.

Summary Findings

During a 12-month period an estimated 14 in every 1,000 persons age 18 or older were victims of stalking

- About half (46 percent) of stalking victims experienced at least one unwanted contact per week, and 11% of victims said they had been stalked for 5 years or more.
- The risk of stalking victimization was highest for individuals who were divorced or separated—34 per 1,000 individuals.
- Women were at greater risk than men for stalking victimization; however, women and men were equally likely to experience harassment.
- Male (37 percent) and female (41 percent) stalking victimizations were equally likely to be reported to the police.

- Approximately 1 in 4 stalking victims reported some form of cyberstalking such as e-mail (83percent) or instant messaging (35 percent).
- 46 percent of stalking victims felt fear of not knowing what would happen next.
- Nearly 3 in 4 stalking victims knew their offender in some capacity.
- More than half of stalking victims lost five or more days from work.
- Bureau of Justice Statistics http://www.bjs.gov/index.cfm?ty=tp&tid=973

96498054R00155

Made in the USA
Columbia, SC
28 May 2018